ALL THAT
GLISTERS...

ALL THAT GLISTERS...

And Other Quotations You Should Know

CAROLINE TAGGART

MICHAEL O'MARA BOOKS LIMITED

First published in Great Britain in 2018 by
Michael O'Mara Books Limited
9 Lion Yard
Tremadoc Road
London SW4 7NQ

A CIP catalogue record for this book is available from the
British Library.

Papers used by Michael O'Mara Books Limited are natural,
recyclable products made from wood grown in sustainable forests.
The manufacturing processes conform to the environmental
regulations of the country of origin.

ISBN: 978-1-78243-997-4 in hardback print format
ISBN: 978-1-78929-002-8 in ebook format

1 2 3 4 5 6 7 8 9 10

Designed and typeset by K.DESIGN, Winscombe, Somerset
Printed and bound by CPI Group (UK) Ltd, Croydon, CR0 4YY

www.mombooks.com

Contents

INTRODUCTION

A few years ago, I wrote a book called *500 Words You Should Know* and chose what to include on the basis that each entry made me think, 'Ooh, that's a nice word.' *All That Glisters . . .* follows the same route for quotations. There are innumerable dictionaries available for those who want to know whether Shakespeare or Emerson originated a certain phrase, or to find a suitable quotation on any given subject to include in a speech. What I have tried to do here is find sayings that appealed to me and that I hope might appeal to you; sayings that might be worked into conversation and make you sound clever, or sympathetic, or worldly wise, depending on the circumstances.

Many of the quotations will be familiar – the pronouncements of Winston Churchill and Abraham Lincoln, inspiration from Maya Angelou and Toni Morrison, smart remarks from Oscar Wilde and Dorothy Parker. A handful are 'attributed to' whoever it may be: it is generally believed – and repeated from website to website – that, say, Mark Twain or George Bernard Shaw wrote a particular *bon mot*, but no one can find the exact source. Too bad, I have said to myself. If it's a good line, let's have it.

Others of my chosen quotations are less well known. Logan Pearsall Smith, H. L. Mencken and the Duc de La Rochefoucauld may no longer be household names, but they spent their lives collecting maxims and coming up with witticisms that will give you something sarcastic or philosophical to say on almost any subject from death to democracy. And some are simply lines that I came across in the course of my own reading as I was researching the book: I don't think Pat Barker's *Like asking Dracula if he had blood* in response to a request for *Whisky, if you have it* has made it into any dictionary of quotations, but I couldn't resist it.

Some personal favourites have crept in, too. I have a weakness for the Roman poet Horace (*No poems can live long or please that are written by water-drinkers*), the politician and writer A. P. Herbert (*A lack of spirit only to be admired in sheep*) and the classic film *Casablanca* (*I think this is the beginning of a beautiful friendship*).

As I did my research, it became clear that, as with proverbs, many quotations contradict each other and therefore back up conflicting points of view. Just as *Fortune favours the brave* encourages the intrepid and *Look before you leap* appeals to the cautious, so, for example, Sir Joshua Reynolds believes in hard work (*You must have no dependence on your own genius. If you have great talents, industry will improve them*) while another painter, Edouard Manet, prefers flair (*Science is all very well, but for us imagination is worth far more*). Look hard enough, in other words, and you will find a quotation to support whatever opinion you care to express.

Having said that, and given that the shortest of formal dictionaries of quotations run to well over 500 pages, a book like this can't possibly claim to be comprehensive. So if you feel I have included too much of one source and not enough of another, I can only say, 'You may be right' and point you to the words of André Maurois quoted in the text: *In literature as in love, we are astonished at what is chosen by others.*

Note: A depressing number of my chosen quotations use the word *man* either to embrace all of humankind or because the originators assumed that only a male had the intellect, the interest or the opportunity to do whatever it was they were talking about. In the context of this book, I didn't feel it was right to alter the wording but, as I have said in some of the relevant entries, I hope you will feel free to adapt the original to embrace any gender or none, to suit your own purposes.

I

BE A BUSH IF YOU CAN'T
BE A TREE

*To begin at the beginning ... here are some thoughts on the
meaning of life, on what makes us tick and what, perhaps, we
should do about it.*

All human misery comes only from this: that we are incapable of remaining quietly in our rooms

An observation by the seventeenth-century French philosopher Blaise Pascal, worth knowing if you want to contradict the many people who have claimed that life is all about taking risks (AVOIDING DANGER IS NO SAFER IN THE LONG RUN THAN OUTRIGHT EXPOSURE, see page 81).

See also page 110: IF CLEOPATRA'S NOSE HAD BEEN SHORTER, THE WHOLE HISTORY OF THE WORLD WOULD HAVE BEEN DIFFERENT.

Anythin' for a quiet life, as the man said when he took the situation at the lighthouse

Sam Weller, Mr Pickwick's faithful servant in Dickens' *Pickwick Papers*, has his own way of expressing things and the book is full of 'Wellerisms' along these lines. In British English the cliché *As the actress said to the bishop* adds innuendo to an innocent but possibly carelessly phrased remark such as *That should slot in quite easily*. The expression had a new lease of life during the run of the TV sitcom *The Office*, in which the character David Brent frequently used it to make inappropriate risqué jokes. The same is true of the American equivalent, *That's what she said* – in the American version of *The Office*, it became a catchphrase of Michael Scott's in response to lines such as *And you were directly under her the entire time*.

But there's no sexual undertone to Sam Weller's remarks – they're just convoluted ways of making a joke, and in his idiosyncratically spelled vernacular, too:

> *The next question is, what the devil do you want with me, as the man said, wen he see the ghost?*

> *That's what I call a self-evident proposition, as the dog's-meat man said, when the housemaid told him he warn't a gentleman.*

> *Vich I call addin' insult to injury, as the parrot said ven they not only took him from his native land, but made him talk the English langwidge arterwards.*

Try making up your own – you'll annoy a gratifying number of people.

Be a bush if you can't be a tree

Six months before he was assassinated in 1968, the civil rights leader Martin Luther King Jr addressed the students of a junior high school in Philadelphia on the subject of 'What is Your Life's Blueprint?' He quoted these oft-repeated lines from Ralph Waldo Emerson:

> *If a man can write a better book or preach a better sermon or make a better mousetrap than his neighbour, even if he builds his house in the woods, the world will make a beaten path to his door.*

Dr King then went on to his own version of the same thought:

> *Be a bush if you can't be a tree. If you can't be a highway, just be a trail. If you can't be a sun, be a star. For it isn't by size that you win or fail. Be the best of whatever you are.*

Many people have extolled the virtue not necessarily of excellence but of doing the very best you can with your talents. As the French philosopher Voltaire put it a couple of centuries earlier:

> *The best is the enemy of the good.*

Or, more recently, H. Jackson Brown Jr, author of *Life's Little Instruction Book*:

> *If you're doing your best, you won't have time to worry about failure.*

Brown is worth quoting further because he achieves the rare feat of working a cephalopod into an inspirational quote:

Talent without discipline is like an octopus on roller skates. There's plenty of movement, but you never know if it's going to be forward, backwards, or sideways.

For another bizarre reference to wildlife, see page 82: BETTER BY FAR YOU SHOULD FORGET AND SMILE THAN THAT YOU SHOULD REMEMBER AND BE SAD, and for more from Emerson see page 33: THOUGH WE TRAVEL THE WORLD OVER TO FIND THE BEAUTIFUL, WE MUST CARRY IT WITH US OR WE FIND IT NOT.

❦

The game is afoot!

Said by Sir Arthur Conan Doyle's Sherlock Holmes in 'The Adventure of the Abbey Grange', as he shakes Dr Watson awake at the start of the story, having been summoned to what sounds like an exciting case. 'The game' isn't a game in the sense of football or Snakes and Ladders; it means the sort of game hunters chase. In Shakespeare's *Henry IV Part I*, the Earl of Northumberland, trying to calm down his hot-headed son, says, *Before the game's a-foot, thou still let'st slip* – meaning, you let the hounds loose before there is any prey for them to run after; you rush into things without thinking.

So Sherlock Holmes means, 'There is something for us to chase.' Is he quoting Shakespeare? Difficult to be sure. But you'll certainly impress a few people if you make the connection.

I can resist everything except temptation

A useful remark for the next time someone offers you a cream cake or a gin and tonic, this comes from Oscar Wilde's *Lady Windermere's Fan*: it's said by Lord Darlington after Lady Windermere has rebuked him for paying her a compliment. The audience already knows that Lord Darlington is not to be taken seriously: Lady Windermere has accused him of being better than most other men but pretending to be worse, to which he replies:

> *So many conceited people go about Society pretending to be good, that I think it shows rather a sweet and modest disposition to pretend to be bad.*

Wilde's plays often feature a young male character pretending to be worse than he is – and he is given some of the best lines. Later in *Lady Windermere's Fan*, Lord Darlington, having fallen in love with the virtuous Lady Windermere, knows he has something fine to aspire to:

> *We are all in the gutter, but some of us are looking at the stars.*

It is also he who gives Wilde's famous definition of a cynic:

> *A man who knows the price of everything and the value of nothing . . .*

. . . the riposte to which, from a character who is accusing Darlington of being sentimental, deserves to be better known:

> *A sentimentalist, my dear Darlington, is a man who sees an absurd value in everything, and doesn't know the market price of any single thing.*

See page 56, I ALWAYS PASS ON GOOD ADVICE, for another of Wilde's cynics. And, to revert to the subject of temptation, Rita Mae Brown (IF IT WEREN'T FOR THE LAST MINUTE, NOTHING WOULD GET DONE, see page 61) seems to have had much the same idea as Lord Darlington:

> Lead me not into temptation; I can find the way myself.

❧

If I am out of my mind, it's all right with me

These are the opening words of Saul Bellow's award-winning novel *Herzog*, and it's the hero, Moses Herzog, who is thinking them. He has in the past wondered if he might be losing his mind, but he feels as if he has come through it: for the moment he's *confident, cheerful, clairvoyant and strong*. As this is page one of a book of almost 400 pages, you can guess it isn't going to be as easy as that – confident and cheerful maybe; clairvoyant not quite so much – but if he has to be out of his mind, he might as well be positive about it.

❧

If one is a greyhound, why try to look like a Pekingese?

'Why not be yourself?' is what the poet Edith Sitwell was trying to say. With a strikingly prominent nose, a quizzical stare and a penchant for huge, eye-catching hats, she certainly made no attempt to look like a Pekingese – or

16

a greyhound, come to that. As she also put it, *I wouldn't dream of following a fashion . . . how could one be a different person every three months?*

If you cannot catch the bird of paradise, better take a wet hen

Spoken by Nikita Khrushchev, leader of the Soviet Union during the 1950s and '60s, and quoted in *Time* on 6 January 1958, when it had just proclaimed him the magazine's Man of the Year for 1957. The remark was Khrushchev's pragmatic response to the failure of some of his agricultural policies. He'd grown up in a farming community and knew that you sometimes had to take the rough with the smooth.

Like Henry Kissinger (THERE CANNOT BE A CRISIS NEXT WEEK. MY SCHEDULE IS ALREADY FULL, see page 176), Khrushchev built up a reputation for 'quotable quotes'. In response to Westerners who claimed that his post-Stalin policies could be used to topple the Soviet Empire, he retorted:

> *You will no more succeed in this than you will succeed in seeing your ear without a mirror.*

And, warning the Czechs to look out for themselves under the new regime:

> *When you walk among dogs, don't forget to carry a stick. After all, that is what a hound has teeth for, to bite when he feels like it.*

If you shed tears when you miss the sun, you also miss the stars

The Indian poet Rabindranath Tagore came up with a wealth of beautiful ways of suggesting that we appreciate the small things of life. This is one of them, but there is also:

> *In the world's audience hall, the simple blade of grass sits on the same carpet with the sunbeams, and the stars of midnight.*

And:

> *The wise man warns me that life is but a dewdrop on the lotus leaf.*

In addition, he had these sage words for those who are only too ready to rush into speech:

> *To be outspoken is easy when you do not wait to speak the complete truth.*

❦

It's more than true. It's a fact

In Harold Pinter's play *The Birthday Party* (sometimes described as a 'comedy of menace'), two sinister strangers, Goldberg and McCann, turn up at a rundown seaside boarding house. As they look around them and get their bearings, Goldberg asks McCann why he seems to be so miserable these days:

> *Everywhere you go these days, it's like a funeral.*
> *That's true.*
> *True? Of course it's true. It's more than true. It's a*
> *fact.*

We don't yet know that these two strangers are sinister – they've only just arrived – but this exchange gives us the first inkling. Goldberg's remark manages to be didactic, threatening and more or less meaningless all at the same time. A useful trick if you can pull it off.

I've a feeling we're not in Kansas any more

This is Dorothy in *The Wizard of Oz*, having – in the 1939 film – just been blown from her black and white rural home to the glorious Technicolor of Oz. A handy expression for any time you are metaphorically blown away by a new sight or experience.

Let me live, love, and say it well in good sentences

Not a bad ambition for any writer, this was the wish of the tragically short-lived poet Sylvia Plath. If you're an aspiring writer, there is an argument that you should be able to make up your own precepts on the subject, but here are a few to tide you over until inspiration strikes.

Perhaps most famously, Virginia Woolf came up with the realistic assessment:

A woman must have money and a room of her own if she is to write fiction.

Iris Murdoch (THE BICYCLE IS THE MOST CIVILIZED CONVEYANCE KNOWN TO MAN, see page 48) also took a pragmatic view of writing as a career:

Writing is like getting married. One should never commit oneself until one is amazed at one's luck.

While Ernest Hemingway was more concerned with an author's ability to assess the value of his or her own work:

The most essential gift for a good writer is a built-in, shock-proof shit detector. This is the writer's radar and all great writers have had it.

He'd surely have approved of the seventeenth-century Frenchman Nicolas Boileau:

Of every four words I write, I strike out three.

A lie can travel half way around the world while the truth is putting on its shoes

This remark is often attributed to Mark Twain, who died in 1910. It's intriguing to speculate on what he might have said had he lived in the age of social media and fake news.

Two centuries earlier, the Irish satirist Jonathan Swift had written a more long-winded version of the same sentiment:

Besides, as the vilest Writer has his Readers, so the greatest Liar has his Believers; and it often happens, that if a Lie be believ'd only for an Hour, it has done its Work, and there is no farther occasion for it. Falsehood flies, and the Truth comes limping after it; so that when Men come to be undeceiv'd, it is too late.

Mud sticks, in other words, and there is no smoke . . .

The novelist Muriel Spark maintained that she wrote her own version of her life story to contradict the many 'strange and erroneous' things that had been written about her. Her take on this sentiment was:

Lies are like fleas hopping from here to there, sucking the blood of the intellect.

In these days of 'saw it on the internet, so it must be true', her words are more pertinent than ever.

❧

Life is always a tightrope or a feather bed . . .

. . . give me the tightrope.
The American novelist and feminist Edith Wharton, writing in the late nineteenth and early twentieth centuries (and the first woman to be awarded the Pulitzer Prize for Literature), clearly didn't want to be bored, which was the lot of most upper-class women of her era. At a time when the sole aim in life for most young ladies was to 'marry well', she wrote not only the words quoted above but also:

I don't know if I should care for a man who made life easy; I should want someone who made it interesting.

And:

> *Beware of monotony: it's the mother of all the deadly sins.*

Given that she was writing many decades before the women's movement took off, you have to admire her spirit.

The main thing is to keep the main thing the main thing

This may seem, at first glance, like the sort of slickly phrased slogan beloved of motivational speakers. But Stephen Covey, author of *The 7 Habits of Highly Effective People*, who came up with it, said a number of things worth pondering. Consider:

> *If we keep doing what we're doing, we're going to keep getting what we're getting.*

> *The more people rationalize cheating, the more it becomes a culture of dishonesty. And that can become a vicious, downward cycle. Because suddenly, if everyone else is cheating, you feel a need to cheat, too.*

And – something to think about in the dark reaches of the night –

> *If you carefully consider what you want to be said of you in the funeral experience, you will find your definition of success.*

On the subject of your own funeral, you may empathize with the ever morose Garrison Keillor:

They say such nice things about people at their funerals that it makes me sad that I'm going to miss mine by just a few days.

❦

Men are always ready to die for us, but not to make our lives worth having

Louisa May Alcott is best known as the author of *Little Women* and this line comes from one of that novel's sequels, *Jo's Boys*. It occurs in a debate about women's suffrage, which must have been quite daring when the book was published in 1886. The female character who speaks it is replying to a young man who has just said that he is prepared to die for women if it will help the cause, a remark that she rightly dismisses as *cheap sentiment and bad logic.*

❦

More ways of killing a cat than choking her with cream

Most of us would say, 'There's more than one way to skin a cat' meaning 'There's more than one way of achieving one's aim'. This variation comes from Charles Kingsley's 1855 novel *Westward Ho!*, a title that, in Kingsley's original conception, meant something like 'Go west, young man'. (It was after the novel's phenomenal success that Westward Ho! became the name first of a hotel and then of the village in Devon where the book was set.)

Kingsley's hero Amyas is serving with Sir Walter Raleigh's fleet, fighting the Spaniards, and employs this expression in a discussion of tactics, advising his men not to rush into things until they have considered all the options. He's obviously using it as a familiar idiom; if you think it is hard on cats, you can console yourself with the thought that it probably originally meant a catfish. Or use another early variant, 'There's more ways of killing the dog than choking him with pudding.'

For more about cats and dogs, see page 67: THE MORE I SEE OF PEOPLE, THE MORE I LIKE DOGS.

Never have a mission, my dear child

Mrs Jellyby, in Dickens' *Bleak House*, does have a mission: she is deeply concerned with the wellbeing of the natives of Borrioboola-Gha, on the left bank of the Niger. Her concern takes the form of a vast amount of letter-writing, speech-making and tea-drinking and leads her to neglect her own family entirely. The advice not to have a mission is given by Mr Jellyby to his daughter Caddy, who is about to be married; the narrator, Esther, remarks that this is the first time she has ever heard him say three words together. Normally he just sits with his head against the wall, a picture of despair. A pitiful warning against misplaced enthusiasm.

No guilty man is acquitted if judged by himself

This is the Roman poet Juvenal on the subject of conscience: he described being judged by yourself as *the first of punishments*. Juvenal was known for his biting satires on life during the Roman Empire – he invented the expression *bread and circuses* as an indictment of the way the masses had lost interest in important issues and now cared only for food and entertainment. He also came up with the unanswerable question *Who will guard the guardians themselves?* in the context of a jealous husband who locks up his wife to prevent her committing adultery, but whose efforts become ridiculous if she takes a fancy to the guards. To sum up, you can't trust anybody.

As for conscience, the great Protestant theologian Martin Luther would have agreed wholeheartedly with Juvenal; he expressed the thought as:

> *I am more afraid of my own heart than of the pope and all his cardinals. I have within me the great pope, Self.*

And, as we shall see under THE BALLOT IS STRONGER THAN THE BULLET (see page 155), you can always rely on H. L. Mencken for the wisecracking version:

> *Conscience is the inner voice that warns us that someone may be looking.*

People would miss out on so many wonderful things if they only stuck with what they knew

A clarion call for taking a few risks. This comes from Rachel Joyce's novel *The Music Shop*, in which Frank, who owns the shop of the title and refuses to sell anything but vinyl, spends his time listening to his customers' problems and recommending records he thinks will help them. He prescribes Aretha Franklin for a man who likes only Chopin and 'Wild Thing' by the Troggs for a sleepless baby; in doing so, he changes lives. This is a man who can think outside the box.

See also page 81: AVOIDING DANGER IS NO SAFER IN THE LONG RUN THAN OUTRIGHT EXPOSURE.

Pity the meek, for they shall inherit the earth

Christ's Sermon on the Mount (see THREE MAY KEEP A SECRET, IF TWO OF THEM ARE DEAD, page 75) includes a list of statements known as the Beatitudes, because they begin with the word 'blessed'. Of these, probably the best known is *Blessed are the meek; for they shall inherit the earth*, a statement that over the centuries has produced any number of satirical observations along the lines of *as long as no one else minds*. The words quoted above, from the American humourist and journalist Don Marquis, take the idea to its logical conclusion: not only are the meek going to inherit a humdinger of a mess, but they are the last people in the world likely to be able or eager to deal with it.

Marquis is best remembered for having created the characters Archy and Mehitabel, a cockroach and an alley cat respectively, and for the fact that Archy recorded their adventures entirely in lower-case characters (because he couldn't press down two keys on the typewriter at once, which in the 1920s and '30s was necessary if you wanted to produce capital letters). The *random thoughts of archy* – who frequently wrote in free verse – are well worth dipping into. They include:

> *boss there is always*
> *a comforting thought*
> *in time of trouble when*
> *it is not our trouble*
>
> *honesty is a good*
> *thing but*
> *it is not profitable to*
> *its possessor*
> *unless it is*
> *kept under control*

And:

> *i have noticed that when chickens quit quarrelling over*
> *their food they often find that there is enough for all*
> *of them i wonder if it might not be the same with the*
> *human race*

Not bad for a cockroach.

Put all your eggs in the one basket – and WATCH THAT BASKET

Each chapter of Mark Twain's *The Tragedy of Pudd'nhead Wilson* is headed by extracts from the *whimsical almanac* that the title character has been compiling for his amusement – *a calendar, with a little dab of ostensible philosophy, usually in ironical form, appended to each date.* The words quoted above are part of one of these little dabs; in full, it reads:

> *Behold, the fool saith, 'Put not all thine eggs in the one basket' – which is but a manner of saying, 'Scatter your money and your attention'; but the wise man saith, 'Put all your eggs in the one basket – and WATCH THAT BASKET.'*

They are eminently quotable, these maxims of Pudd'nhead's:

> *Nothing so needs reforming as other people's habits.*

> *If you pick up a starving dog and make him prosperous, he will not bite you. This is the principal difference between a dog and a man.*

> *Few things are harder to put up with than the annoyance of a good example.*

And, more whimsically:

> *Thanksgiving Day. Let all give humble, hearty, and sincere thanks, now, but the turkeys. In the island of Fiji they do not use turkeys; they use plumbers. It does not become you and me to sneer at Fiji.*

With two of these to most chapters and a total of twenty-one chapters, there is enough cod philosophy to last a short lifetime and to suit most purposes.

See also page 119: THERE IS A CHARM ABOUT THE FORBIDDEN THAT MAKES IT UNSPEAKABLY DESIRABLE.

Reserve your right to think, for even to think wrongly is better than not to think at all

These words are attributed to Hypatia of Alexandria, one of the earliest known female mathematicians. She lived in the fourth and fifth centuries AD and none of her writings have come down to us, so it's difficult to be sure what she *did* write, but this thought is worth remembering anyway.

Two other great thinkers expressed approval not only of thinking *per se*, but of the right to change your mind. The Roman Emperor Marcus Aurelius, writing two and a half centuries before Hypatia, believed:

> *To change your mind and to follow him who sets you right is to be nonetheless the free agent that you were before.*

And nearly two millennia later, Ralph Waldo Emerson was advising:

> *A foolish consistency is the hobgoblin of little minds … Speak what you think to-day in words as hard as cannon-balls, and to-morrow speak what to-morrow thinks in hard words again, though it contradict every thing you said to-day.*

Alexander Pope, however, not given to self-doubt, was all for sticking to your guns. In his *Essay on Criticism* (To ERR IS HUMAN, TO FORGIVE DIVINE, see page 34), he wrote disparagingly of those who were easily persuaded:

> *Some praise at morning what they blame at night;*
> *But always think the last opinion right.*

❦

A rose by any other name

This is the commonly used abridged version of lines from the famous 'balcony scene' in Shakespeare's *Romeo and Juliet*. Juliet has just discovered that the man she has fallen in love with belongs to the Montague family, her own family's enemies. Not knowing that Romeo is within earshot in the garden below, she wonders aloud, *Romeo, Romeo, wherefore art thou Romeo?* – with wherefore, of course, meaning why rather than where. She goes on:

> *'Tis but thy name that is my enemy.*
> *Thou art thyself, though, not a Montague.*
> *What's Montague? It is nor hand, nor foot,*
> *Nor arm, nor face, nor any other part*
> *Belonging to a man. O, be some other name!*
> *What's in a name? That which we call a rose*
> *By any other name would smell as sweet.*

Young Mr Montague, she concludes, would still be the wonderful person he is if he weren't called Montague. None of this makes any difference to the tragic outcome of the play but the expression is useful if you want to indicate that changing something's name is purely cosmetic and doesn't make any material difference.

❦

Run and find out

This, according to Rudyard Kipling's *The Jungle Book*, is the motto of the mongoose family:

> *It is the hardest thing in the world to frighten a mongoose, because he is eaten up from nose to tail with curiosity.*

Kipling's mongoose, Rikki-tikki-tavi, is not only curious, he is brave and loyal, sprightly and cunning; and he is a true friend to the human family who have adopted him, defending them from the venomous snakes in the garden. Never mind *Curiosity killed the cat* – that's the sort of thing Victorian nannies used to say to frighten children. *Curiosity saved the mongoose* is a much more exciting motto.

❦

The sentimentalist ages far more quickly than the person who loves his work and enjoys new challenges

So said the actress Lillie Langtry, best known as the mistress of the future King Edward VII, son of Queen Victoria, although their affair lasted only three years and, for both parties, was one of many. Lillie had a varied career during which she, at different times, owned a racing stable and a vineyard and put her famously lovely complexion to profitable use advertising Pears' soap; she then grew old more gracefully than many ageing beauties, maintaining that:

> *Anyone who limits her vision to memories of yesterday is already dead.*

Bizarrely, given her headline-grabbing lifestyle, as a young woman Lillie became friendly with the eminently respectable Prime Minister William Gladstone, over forty years her senior, and he gave her a sound piece of advice on her burgeoning acting career. Warning her that, as someone in the public eye, she would be open to all sorts of just and unjust criticism, he told her never to respond to it:

> *Above all, never rush into print to explain or defend yourself.*

That's a thought that many users of social media today would do well to consider.

There is nothing new under the sun

To put it more fully:

> *What has happened will happen again, and what has been done will be done again, and there is nothing new under the sun.*

That isn't even putting it very fully – there is a lot more in this vein; the passage begins with the famous words *Vanity of vanities; all is vanity.*

It's from the first chapter of the Old Testament book of Ecclesiastes, which is frankly pretty gloomy. We're always looking for novelty, it says, coming up with new inventions, but there is no such thing: we're just drawing on what God has already thought of. Things that have happened (and people who have lived) in the past are soon forgotten and the whole same-old-same-old starts all over again.

So this is a world-weary thing to say, and can be capped by another verse from the same chapter:

> *For in much wisdom is much grief: and he that increaseth knowledge increaseth sorrow.*

Not necessarily something you want to try on a teacher at school when you haven't done your homework.

❦

Though we travel the world over to find the beautiful, we must carry it with us or we find it not

An idea that is popular with many poets and philosophers: what you get out of life depends on what you put in to it. This is Ralph Waldo Emerson's take on HE WHO HAS NO POETRY IN HIMSELF WILL FIND POETRY IN NOTHING, see page 163, and it isn't far removed from Louisa May Alcott's view:

> *It's amazing how lovely common things become, if one only knows how to look at them.*

For more of her wise words, see page 23: MEN ARE ALWAYS READY TO DIE FOR US, BUT NOT TO MAKE OUR LIVES WORTH HAVING.

To err is human, to forgive divine

This is so commonly quoted that it has attained proverbial status, but in fact it's a line from Alexander Pope's 'didactic poem' *An Essay on Criticism*, published in 1711. Pope is writing – critically – about the writer's longing for praise and the critic's tendency to be unkind, advocating that *Good-nature and good sense must ever join*. Thus the point is not that the ability to forgive is God's prerogative – it's that it's a godly quality to which we should all aspire.

Like George Bernard Shaw (IN HEAVEN AN ANGEL IS NOBODY IN PARTICULAR, see page 63), Pope rather self-consciously wrote quotable one-liners: *Fools rush in where angels fear to tread* also comes from the *Essay on Criticism* and *Hope springs eternal in the human breast* is from his *Essay on Man*.

Two men look out through the same bars; one sees the mud, and one the stars

It's all a question of attitude. This is from *A Cluster of Quiet Thoughts* by the nineteenth-century Irish churchman Frederick Langbridge; the English poet Richard Lovelace had remarked 250 years earlier:

> *Stone walls do not a prison make,*
> *Nor iron bars a cage.*

While in the twentieth century, G. K. Chesterton wrote, of the rolling English drunkard who made the rolling English road, that:

> *... the wild rose was above him when they found him in the ditch.*

You can find good in any situation, these writers are saying – even if, like Chesterton's hero, you are more than a little the worse for wear.

What does not kill me makes me stronger

A line from the philosopher Friedrich Nietzsche, which he preceded with the words *From life's school of war*. In other words, this is a lesson learned over the years. It has been much quoted and paraphrased, so you may choose to take the darker view expressed in song by Marilyn Manson:

> *Whatever doesn't kill you is gonna leave a scar.*

Or the weirder one from the Joker in the film *The Dark Knight*:

> *What doesn't kill you simply makes you stranger.*

Like many philosophers, Nietzsche had an ear for a neat turn of phrase.

> *There is always some madness in love. But there is also always some reason in madness.*

And:

> *It is not a lack of love, but a lack of friendship that makes unhappy marriages ...*

... are two that you could debate long into the night. Throw in the observation that Nietzsche never married and you can begin to wonder if he knew as much about the subject as, say, P. G. Wodehouse (CHUMPS ALWAYS MAKE THE BEST HUSBANDS, see page 107).

What the caterpillar calls the end of the world, the master calls a butterfly

You could take this as a suggestion that you should always look on the bright side of life, or a neutral statement that everything depends on how you look at it (see page 34, TWO MEN LOOK OUT THROUGH THE SAME BARS, for more on the latter theme). It's from *Illusions: The Adventures of a Reluctant Messiah* by American philosopher Richard Bach. Bach's most famous work, *Jonathan Livingston Seagull*, is full of metaphors about flying, freedom and achieving dreams. Try:

> *You didn't need faith to fly, you needed to understand flying.*

Or:

> *His sorrow was not solitude, it was that other gulls refused to believe the glory of flight that awaited them; they refused to open their eyes and see.*

When a man does not know what harbour he is making for, no wind is the right wind

This is the Roman philosopher Seneca the Younger, writing in the first century AD. What he means, of course, is 'How can you achieve what you want if you don't know what that is?' If you are an artist rather than a sailor, you can (as Seneca did) put it this way:

> *The artist may have his colours all prepared, but he cannot produce a likeness unless he has already made up his mind what he wishes to paint.*

Whichever career path you choose to use as your example, the idea is that you should make up your mind what you want to do and then get on with it.

Whoever would be cured of ignorance must first confess it

The maxims of the sixteenth-century French essayist Michel de Montaigne could fill a book on their own. His best known is probably:

> *When I play with my cat, who knows whether she is passing the time with me more than I am with her?*

But there is also:

> *Fame and tranquillity can never live under the same roof.*

And:

> *However much we may mount on stilts, we still must walk on our own legs. And on the highest throne in the world, we still sit only on our own backside.*

Montaigne favoured sitting at home with lots of good books and living a quiet life; if you need ways of dealing with someone getting above themselves, make him your first port of call.

❦

Wise men speak because they have something to say...

...fools because they have to say something.

This is often attributed to Plato, but it's unlikely that he said it, not least because the play on words of *have* (meaning to possess) and *have to* (to be obliged to) doesn't work in Ancient Greek.

The academic and theologian Richard Whately, in his 1828 *Elements of Rhetoric*, expressed the same thought rather more verbosely:

> *Universally, a writer or speaker should endeavour to maintain the appearance of expressing himself, not, as if he wanted to say something, but as if he had something to say: i.e. not as if he had a subject set him, and was anxious to compose the best essay or declamation on it that he could; but as if he had some ideas to which he was anxious to give utterance; – not as if he wanted to compose (for instance) a sermon, and was desirous of performing that task satisfactorily...*

... and so on. OK, Richard, thank you, I think we get the idea.

The French novelist Stendhal (IT'S IMPOSSIBLE TO GET ALONG WITH SOMEONE WHO IS ALWAYS RIGHT, see page 63) had an interesting take on the same theme:

> *When you impose silence on yourself you discover ideas; when you make it a rule to talk, you find nothing to say.*

The idea that it is better to remain silent and be thought a fool than to open one's mouth and remove all doubt has, like many other witticisms, been credited to both Mark Twain and Abraham Lincoln; it is also attributed to an American writer called Maurice Switzer, who included it in an anthology of doggerel and nursery-rhyme parodies called *Mrs Goose, Her Book* (though he was almost certainly quoting an earlier source). So no one is sure where exactly it came from. But it echoes a verse from the biblical book of Proverbs:

> *Even a fool, when he holdeth his peace, is counted wise: and he that shutteth his lips is esteemed a man of understanding.*

Whoever you choose to quote in this context, the moral is to keep quiet until you know what you are talking about.

A word, once released, cannot be called back again

This is the Roman poet Horace's warning against gossip. Be careful what you say, he advises, and be careful to whom you say it: someone who pesters you with questions is almost certainly burning to pass on anything you tell them. Make sure that anyone you recommend is worthy of your good opinion, too: if they turn out not to be, your own reputation will be tarnished. As one translation puts it:

> *It is your own interest that is at stake when your neighbour's wall is on fire.*

Prudent advice, perhaps, but not very exciting. Horace is more fun than this makes him sound – see NO POEMS CAN LIVE LONG OR PLEASE THAT ARE WRITTEN BY WATER-DRINKERS for his views on drink and YOU MAY DRIVE OUT NATURE WITH A PITCHFORK, YET SHE STILL WILL HURRY BACK for him on the subject of gardening (see pages 173 and 180).

Wouldn't it be possible for us just to banish these men from our lives, and escape their carping and jeering once and for all?

One of the earliest pieces of feminist writing appeared in sixteenth-century Venice, the work of a highly educated woman called Moderata Fonte and entitled *The Worth of Women*. Perhaps feeling that the title wasn't clear enough, she set the tone for the rest of the book by adding a subtitle: *Wherein Is Clearly Revealed Their Nobility and Their Superiority to Men.*

Moderata seems to have had a very happy marriage, but to have objected generally to the patronizing way in which men treat women, apparently blind to women's virtues and intelligence. Dismissing what historians tell us about men and women, she points out that histories have been written by men, *who never tell the truth except by accident,* and goes on to discuss women's place in society:

> *When it's said that women must be subject to men, the phrase should be understood in the same sense as when we say we are subject to natural disasters, diseases, and all the other accidents of this life: it's not a case of being subjected in the sense of obeying, but rather of suffering an imposition, not a case of serving them fearfully, but rather of tolerating them in a spirit of Christian charity, since they have been given to us by God as a spiritual trial.*

There is plenty more in the same vein if the general intolerability of the male sex is a theme that arouses your interest.

2

BEWARE OF ALL ENTERPRISES
THAT REQUIRE NEW CLOTHES

Rubbing along together – what people have had to say on society, religion and the art of conversation.

The absent are always in the wrong

Hardly an original sentiment, but coined in this form by the French playwright Philippe Néricault Destouches in *The Unforeseen Obstacle* (1717). The heroine's maid Nérine is explaining that she has fallen in love with the valet of her mistress's suitor – it's what always happens, she says, in plays of this sort. But, in a break with convention, master and servant have gone off to seek their fortune and, although the mistress is waiting constantly, Nérine, finding that *The absent are always in the wrong*, has married someone else. Destouches' comedies tend to mix farce and mistaken identities with a high moral tone (which means they swither uneasily between being a bit silly and not very funny at all), so it's safe to assume he doesn't mean us to take everything Nérine says at face value. Even if he did, it's worth giving thought to Dorothy Parker's views on throwing mud (WHEREVER SHE WENT, INCLUDING HERE, IT WAS AGAINST HER BETTER JUDGEMENT, see page 101).

❧

*A*lea iacta est

There aren't many things that you can get away with saying in Latin – *Carpe diem* is one (see NO POEMS CAN LIVE LONG OR PLEASE THAT ARE WRITTEN BY WATER-DRINKERS, page 173), and these words may just be another. They mean 'the die is cast', there's no going back now. According to the Roman biographer Suetonius, Julius Caesar said this as he was about to cross the river Rubicon, which marked the boundary between Cisalpine Gaul and the Roman Republic. By crossing this border with an army at his back, Caesar committed an act of treason and started off the chain of events that led to the Ides of March and *Et tu, Brute?* – something else you can say in Latin without sounding *too* pretentious.

By the way, Suetonius doesn't record Caesar saying, *Et tu, Brute?* to Brutus when he is murdered; he has *What! art thou, too, one of them? Thou, my son!* – only for some reason he puts it in Greek. Most commentators agree that Shakespeare's shorter, Latin version has more of a ring to it.

❧

43

All animals are equal but some animals are more equal than others

Of course, everyone is equal, but someone still has to be in charge, right? This is the chilling message of George Orwell's *Animal Farm*, which, in an allegory of the Russian Revolution and its aftermath, shows how the ideals of the revolution (in which the animals, led by the pigs, have ousted the humans from the farm) are pitifully short-lived. The revolutionaries start to quarrel among themselves, and to realize the advantages of a privileged position – the pigs take to drinking alcohol and sleeping in beds, two things that were expressly forbidden by the original Seven Commandments of Animalism. Continuing the analogy into the Stalin years, the pigs rewrite the rules they themselves drew up, to suit their new tastes, so the original rules become *No animal shall drink alcohol to excess* and *No animal shall sleep in a bed with sheets*. Most terrifyingly of all, to the commandment *No animal shall kill any other animal* are added the words *without cause*. And when the pigs take to standing on their hind legs, the mantra *Four legs good, two legs bad* somehow becomes *Four legs good, two legs better*.

So the pigs' rewriting of their rule on equality – which of course started out simply as *All animals are equal* – can be drawn into the conversation any time anything is manifestly unfair.

All beginnings are delightful . . .

. . . the threshold is the place to pause.
A charming thought from the German poet Johann Goethe, suggesting that we should wait a moment and contemplate any room – or situation – we are about to enter. It's tempting to wonder if Goethe had love affairs in mind; in that context he also wrote:

> *Love is an ideal thing; marriage is a real thing;*
> *a confusion of the real with the ideal never goes*
> *unpunished.*

Always remember that you are absolutely unique. Just like everyone else

Probably only an anthropologist could have said this; certainly an anthropologist did: Margaret Mead, who studied the indigenous people of Samoa in the early twentieth century and caused a furore by writing about their sex lives. She also, as long ago as 1928, made an observation that will strike a chord with anyone baffled by the array of options in a modern supermarket:

> *A society which is clamouring for choice, which is*
> *filled with many articulate groups, each urging its*
> *own brand of salvation, its own variety of economic*
> *philosophy, will give each new generation no peace*
> *until all have chosen or gone under, unable to bear the*
> *conditions of choice.*

An atheist is a man who has no invisible means of support

Once you get on to the subjects of God and religion, there is no shortage of wisecracks to be made. No one seems to know where this one originated: it's widely credited to John Buchan, author of *The Thirty-Nine Steps*, but when he used it in 1935 he was quoting it as 'something he'd heard'. Still, whatever the source, there's always room for a smart one-liner. More lengthy, but worth reflecting on, is George Orwell's remark in *Down and Out in Paris and London* about a tramp he encounters on his travels:

> *He was an embittered atheist (the sort of atheist who does not so much disbelieve in God as personally dislike Him).*

Orwell – who never quite severed his ties with the Church of England, dabbled with atheism and loathed Catholicism – had obviously given the matter some thought: reviewing the Catholic Graham Greene's novel *The Heart of the Matter* (in which a character does something he believes will lead him to eternal damnation), he wrote that there was 'a sort of snobbishness' in Greene's attitude:

> *He appears to share the idea ... that there is something rather* distingué *in being damned; Hell is a sort of high-class night club, entry to which is reserved for Catholics only, since the others, the non-Catholics, are too ignorant to be held guilty.*

And if Hell can be *distingué*, so, too, can burial. The final word on the subject goes to a committed atheist, the mathematician and philosopher Bertrand Russell, who claimed to have been told that the Chinese were going to bury him with great honour and erect a shrine to his memory:

> *I have some slight regret that this did not happen as I might have become a god, which would have been very chic for an atheist.*

Indeed it would.

❦

Beware of all enterprises that require new clothes

The American essayist and poet Henry David Thoreau (LIVES OF QUIET DESPERATION, see page 90) didn't approve of new clothes:

> *Only they who go to soirées and legislative balls must have new coats, coats to change as often as the man changes in them. But if my jacket and trousers, my hat and shoes, are fit to worship God in, they will do; will they not?*

He clearly didn't go to many soirées or legislative balls. His mentor Ralph Waldo Emerson (THE LOUDER HE TALKED OF HIS HONOUR, THE FASTER WE COUNTED OUR SPOONS, see page 141) was more conventional on the subject:

> *If, however, a man has not firm nerves and has keen sensibility, it is perhaps a wise economy to go to a good shop and dress himself irreproachably. He can then dismiss all care from his mind . . . I have heard with admiring submission the experience of the lady who*

> declared that 'the sense of being perfectly well-dressed
> gives a feeling of inward tranquillity which religion is
> powerless to bestow'.

But Emerson made a large part of his living from lecturing and had to pay some attention to the impression he made on others; Thoreau, immersing himself in the middle of nowhere, a mile from any of his neighbours, could afford not to give a damn.

❧

The bicycle is the most civilized conveyance known to man . . .

. . . Other forms of transport grow daily more nightmarish. Only the bicycle remains pure in heart.
This is the novelist and philosopher Iris Murdoch echoing the sentiments of anyone who has tried to drive in a big city lately. Although she expressed a lot of high-falutin' views on life, love, literature and truth –

> *For most of us, for almost all of us, truth can be attained, if at all, only in silence. It is in silence that the human spirit touches the divine.*

– she wasn't entirely removed from the everyday:

> *One of the secrets of a happy life is continuous small treats, and if some of these can be inexpensive and quickly procured so much the better.*

She'd probably have responded favourably to this idea from the multi-Michelin-star-winning chef Alain Ducasse:

Everywhere in the world there are tensions – economic, political, religious. So we need chocolate.

And it's interesting, in passing, to note that Bertrand Russell – mentioned under AN ATHEIST IS A MAN WHO HAS NO INVISIBLE MEANS OF SUPPORT (see page 46) and, like Murdoch, one of the great intellects of a generation – also recognized the importance of treats. A contemporary at Cambridge recalled that:

In a disquisition on the capacity of mankind for misery he said he had never been so unhappy that he would not have been cheered, in an appreciable measure, by the sudden offer of a chocolate-cream.

❧

Big Brother is watching you

The inspiration for the reality TV show *Big Brother*, this is a line from George Orwell's *Nineteen Eighty-Four*: Big Brother is the head of a totalitarian state that keeps its citizens under surveillance at all times, and the slogan *Big Brother is watching you* is on display everywhere they go.

More frighteningly, Orwell shows that the state – not content with 24/7 surveillance – also gets inside its citizens' heads. It has created the Thought Police, whose job it is to stamp out any signs of individuality or independent thinking; invented a language, Newspeak, to give convenient new meanings to words such as 'free' and 'equal'; and introduced the concept of Doublethink – 'the act of simultaneously accepting two mutually contradictory beliefs as correct'. Another television programme, *Room 101*, takes its title from the *Nineteen Eighty-Four* concept of a room used by the Ministry of Love (whose remit includes the interrogation and torturing of dissidents). In Room 101 a dissident faces 'the worst thing in the world', which varies uncannily from individual to individual.

George Orwell's imagination would have run riot in the age of the smartphone. Think about Big Brother next time you are leaving your local supermarket or coffee shop and you receive a message asking you to 'rate your experience': somebody, somewhere is watching you.

Bliss was it in that dawn to be alive ...

... But to be young was very heaven!
William Wordsworth wrote this in his autobiographical *Prelude* and also in a poem called 'The French Revolution as It Appeared to its Enthusiasts at its Commencement'. An enthusiastic supporter of the Revolution in his youth, Wordsworth became less radical as he turned more of his attention towards daffodils and views from Westminster Bridge. The line nevertheless is a good one for recalling the joys and optimism of youth and for contradicting Dante (THERE IS NO GREATER SORROW THAN TO RECALL A TIME OF HAPPINESS IN MISERY, see page 98). There's no need to go round chopping people's heads off, though.

The Cabots talk only to God

Possibly the only oculist quoted in this book, John Collins Bossidy was a graduate of the Holy Cross College in Boston, and he spoke this verse as a toast at an alumni dinner in 1910:

And this is good old Boston,
The home of the bean and the cod,
Where the Lowells talk to the Cabots
And the Cabots talk only to God.

As this piece of doggerel suggests, Boston was (is?) stereotypically perceived as having a rigid social hierarchy and a considerable sense of its own importance. The jurist Oliver Wendell Holmes Jr, a native of Boston who spent much of his time in Washington DC serving at the Supreme Court, remarked:

It takes me several days, after I get back to Boston, to realize that the reference 'the president' refers to the president of Harvard and not to a minor official in Washington.

Oliver Wendell Holmes Sr, the jurist's father, was a highly regarded poet. Also a resident of Boston, he stuck his neck out about another couple of cities:

Chicago sounds rough to the maker of verse.
One comfort we have – Cincinnati sounds worse.

Come to that, whatever the virtues of Galveston or Amarillo, not many people sing about leaving their heart in Los Angeles, Detroit or Des Moines, Iowa.

Circumstances beyond my individual control

These grandiose words are the beginning of an even more grandiose letter written by Mr Micawber to David Copperfield in Charles Dickens' novel of the same name; what he goes on to say means little more than 'Sorry I haven't been in touch'. If you are in the mood for the grandiloquent and the circumlocutory, Mr Micawber is an excellent source: he writes that his circumstances have taken an unfortunate turn *through his original errors and a fortuitous combination of unpropitious events*; that he has been placed *in a mental position of peculiar painfulness*; and that *Mrs Micawber is not in confidential possession of my intentions*. In other words, things have gone badly, he's upset and he hasn't told his wife he is coming to London for a couple of days. Some unspecified villainy has been responsible for his misfortune, but he may have the opportunity of *wielding the thunderbolt, or directing the devouring and avenging flame*. Never say it in two words if twenty-seven words will do, and never say it directly if you can go all round the houses, those are Mr Micawber's mottos. And these examples are all from the same letter – think how many you'll find in a novel of over a thousand pages.

Even a dead fish can go with the flow

This is attributed to the American journalist and political activist Jim Hightower (though variations are attributed to others, too); in Hightower's case it is an extension of the statement: *The opposite of courage is not cowardice, it is conformity.*

Hightower has an odd affinity to deceased wildlife; he's also quoted as saying:

> *There's nothing in the middle of the road but yellow stripes and dead armadillos.*

Perhaps he just doesn't approve of anyone not taking a stand. And he isn't alone. He would probably agree with the eighteenth- and nineteenth-century English novelist Fanny Burney, who wrote:

> *There is nothing upon the face of the earth so insipid as a medium. Give me love or hate! a friend that will go to jail for me, or an enemy that will run me through the body!*

And, on this evidence, Hightower and Burney would almost certainly share David Lloyd George's disapproval of rival politician John Simon:

> *He has sat on the fence so long that the iron has entered his soul.*

Every action done in company ought to be with some sign of respect to those that are present

When he was a boy the future President George Washington compiled a list of maxims called *The Rules of Civility*; the words quoted above are what Lewis Carroll might have called Rule Number One (It's THE OLDEST RULE IN THE BOOK, see page 168). Washington's 110 rules were taken largely from a Jesuit etiquette manual dating from the sixteenth century and it's believed that he wrote them out merely as a handwriting exercise. They cover such diverse subjects as sitting up straight, caring for your nails, hands and teeth, and not eating in the street, as well as:

> *Undertake not to Teach your equal in the art himself*
> *Professes; it savours of arrogancy.*

And:

> *Be not hasty to believe flying Reports to the*
> *Disparagement of any.*

There is a lot more in this vein – the slightly earnest morality you might expect from a boy who chopped down a cherry tree and then told his father he couldn't tell a lie.

❧

Every body is interested in pigeons

Arguably the worst piece of publishing advice ever given to a budding author (and, as anyone in the business will tell you, *Watership Down*, *The Day of the Jackal* and the first Harry Potter were all turned down by numerous publishers, so they are a breed prone to making short-sighted decisions). These words were offered in 1859 to Charles Darwin's publisher, John Murray, by the editor of the influential *Quarterly Review*, a clergyman called Whitwell Elwin. At Murray's request, Elwin had read the first three chapters of Darwin's *On the Origin of Species* and was worried that the author hadn't put forward enough evidence of his theories to convince

54

a sceptical reading public. He recommended that, instead of giving a wide-ranging survey of natural selection, Darwin focus on pigeons, showing how they illustrated the principles involved. His reason? *Every body is interested in pigeons.*

Mercifully for posterity, Darwin refused to make the proposed amendments and the book he had written was published. If he'd taken the Reverend Elwin's opinion to heart, we'd have been denied one of the most important books in the history of science. As it is, we've missed out on ... a treatise on pigeons.

Every man is surrounded by a neighbourhood of voluntary spies

In Jane Austen's *Northanger Abbey*, young Catherine Morland, her head full of the horrors of Gothic novels, is staying in the sinister abbey of the title, owned by General Tilney. She has convinced herself that the general murdered his wife and is tentatively putting forward this theory to the general's son, Henry. He tries to set her right: remember that we are in England; that there are laws; consider your own sense of what is probable. And, to bring in the words quoted above, bear in mind that, particularly in the country, everyone knows everyone else's business.

Jane Austen knew all about the nosiness of country neighbourhoods; she lived in one for most of her life and in *Pride and Prejudice* she has Mr Bennet express this cynical view:

*For what do we live, but to make sport for our
neighbours, and laugh at them in our turn?*

❧

I always pass on good advice . . .

*. . . It is the only thing to do with it. It is never of any use to
oneself.*

We saw under I CAN RESIST EVERYTHING EXCEPT
TEMPTATION (see page 15) that Oscar Wilde's comedies
often contain a young man who is pretending to be a
worse character than he actually is: on this occasion it is
Lord Goring in *An Ideal Husband*. The advice – which his
father gave him an hour ago and which he is now passing
on to a sprightly young woman called Mabel Chiltern –
is simply to go to bed early (and alone), rather than keep
the decadent hours required by London society. Lord
Goring has no intention of doing anything of the sort
himself, and neither has Mabel, nor anyone else at the
party where this conversation takes place.

❧

I am glad I was not born before tea

Just as the world is divided into dog people and cat people
(THE MORE I SEE OF PEOPLE, THE MORE I LIKE DOGS,
see page 67), so there are tea lovers and coffee lovers. The
nineteenth-century cleric and wit Sydney Smith was one
of the former; he prefaced this remark with:

Thank God for tea! What would the world do without tea! How did it exist?

He was an Englishman, so you'd expect him to rhapsodize about tea, but he does go on to say:

If you want to improve your understanding, drink coffee.

G. K. Chesterton was English, too, with the imperialistic arrogance of his period. His poem 'Song of Right and Wrong' includes the lines:

Tea, although an Oriental,
Is a gentleman at least;
Cocoa is a cad and coward,
Cocoa is a vulgar beast.

The above is a mere sample of Chesterton's extraordinary rant against the hapless cocoa – he obviously disliked it intensely. He also had strong views on wine and soda water, but made no mention of coffee. For that you generally have to rely on the fridge-magnet level of wit – *May your coffee be strong and your Monday be short* or *Coffee keeps me going till it's time for wine.* But the sure-fire way for coffee drinkers to impress is to quote a sixteenth-century sheikh – not something that happens every day. The sheikh in question rejoiced in the name of Ansari Djezeri Hanball Abd-al-Kadir and in 1587 he published a poem called 'In Praise of Coffee' that included the lines:

All Cares vanish as the coffee cup is raised to the lips.
Coffee flows through your body as freely as your life's blood, refreshing all that it touches: look you at the youth and vigour of those who drink it.

Sounds good, certainly, but the sheikh also reckoned that:

> *Whoever tastes coffee will forever forswear the liquor of the grape.*

... So you need to be careful just how far down this path you want to go. Maybe the moderate Sydney Smith, who was not so dedicated to the cause of tea that he refused a glass of wine with his evening meal, is the safer man to follow. For more of his many *bons mots*, see page 71: POVERTY IS NO DISGRACE TO A MAN, BUT IT IS CONFOUNDEDLY INCONVENIENT.

I don't want to belong to any club that will accept me as a member

Although opinions differ over the exact wording, this is the form the comedian Groucho Marx uses in his autobiography and he says the club in question was the Delaney (again, opinions differ). He describes himself as *not a particularly gregarious fellow* to whom clubbableness doesn't come naturally – *After a month or so my mouth aches from baring my teeth in a false smile* – and he tenders his resignation after a particularly ghastly dinner sitting next to a barber who insists on talking about electric razors.

Groucho relates this story in a chapter called 'Foot-in-mouth Disease' and he may have been the first to apply that expression to human conversational blunders. Among his others are his response, when on a trip to

Mexico, to an invitation to meet the President at his palace the following afternoon at four o'clock:

What assurance have I got that he'll still be President by four o'clock tomorrow afternoon?

He also relates filling in a Customs form and giving his occupation as 'smuggler', and explaining to Greta Garbo that he had tipped her hat over her face because he thought she was 'a fellow I knew from Kansas City'. If you're in the habit of making remarks that you regret the moment they are out of your mouth, read Groucho's memoirs and take comfort in the knowledge that you are not alone.

❦

I have often wished I had time to cultivate modesty

The *Observer* newspaper quoted Edith Sitwell (IF ONE IS A GREYHOUND, WHY TRY TO LOOK LIKE A PEKINGESE?, see page 16) as saying these words in 1950, when she was sixty-two and had surely had time to acquire modesty if she wanted to; she added, *But I am too busy thinking about myself.*

There is more than one way of looking at self-esteem. The Victorian novelist Anthony Trollope was all in favour of a bit of conceit:

Nobody holds a good opinion of a man who has a low opinion of himself.

Whereas Anthony Powell, writing nearly a century later, observed that it could be taken too far:

He fell in love with himself at first sight and it is a passion to which he has always remained faithful.

I would rather be a rebel than a slave

You can imagine that the suffragettes of the early twentieth century had many memorable things to say about their cause, but this – from the most prominent of them, Emmeline Pankhurst – is among the pithiest. You may also like:

> *Courage calls to courage everywhere, and its voice cannot be denied ...*

... the first part of which adorns the statue of Millicent Fawcett in Parliament Square in London. Alternatively, if you have time on your hands and want to get into a discussion, you might opt for:

> *People are led to reason thus: a woman who is a wife is one who has made a permanent sex bargain for her maintenance; the woman who is not married must therefore make a temporary bargain of the same kind.*

This last quote is from Christabel Pankhurst, daughter of Emmeline; it's a sentiment shared by her near-contemporary, the author and activist Rebecca West. In remarkably frank language, considering that this was before World War I, West wrote:

> *I myself have never been able to find out precisely what a feminist is; I only know that people call me a feminist*

*whenever I express sentiments that differentiate me
from a doormat or a prostitute.*

And while we are on the subject, here are two similarly
forceful opinions from the French philosopher Simone
de Beauvoir:

*This has always been a man's world, and none of the
reasons that have been offered in explanation have
seemed adequate.*

And:

*Man is defined as a human being and woman as a
female; whenever she behaves like a human being she
is said to be imitating the male.*

Quite.

❧

If it weren't for the last minute, nothing would get done

Just as numerous proverbs contradict each other
(*Many hands make light work/Too many cooks spoil the
broth; Look before you leap/He who hesitates is lost* and
that sort of thing), so do opinions about the evils of
procrastination. These pragmatic words come from the
American writer Rita Mae Brown, and make a refreshing
contrast to the many worthy remarks that have been
made on the subject. At the other end of the scale comes
the American academic Mason Cooley, known for his
aphorisms:

> *Procrastination makes easy things hard, hard things harder.*

And the American President Theodore Roosevelt:

> *In a moment of decision, the best thing you can do is the right thing to do, the next best thing is the wrong thing, and the worst thing you can do is nothing.*

If you really want to be eloquent, though, go for the English essayist Thomas de Quincey, best known for his *Confessions of an English Opium Eater*. In a lesser known work called *Murder Considered as One of the Fine Arts* he gave this detailed guide to the slippery slope towards vice:

> *If once a man indulges himself in murder, very soon he comes to think little of robbing; and from robbing he comes next to drinking and Sabbath-breaking, and from that to incivility and procrastination.*

Next time you have the urge to murder anyone, it's worth pausing to ponder the depths of depravity to which it might lead.

And, before we pass on entirely from Rita Mae Brown, consider this (sometimes attributed in a slightly different form to former First Lady Nancy Reagan):

> *People are like tea bags; you never know how strong they'll be until they're in hot water.*

In heaven an angel is nobody in particular

This statement by George Bernard Shaw comes from a collection of *Maxims for Revolutionists*. It was here that he published perhaps his most notorious precept:

> *He who can, does. He who cannot, teaches.*

But the list also contains advice on politics, education and the vanity of many human ambitions. Almost every line seems to have been written to be quotable, but the more thought-provoking ones include:

> *The man with toothache thinks everyone happy whose teeth are sound. The poverty-stricken man makes the same mistake about the rich man.*

And:

> *In an ugly and unhappy world the richest man can purchase nothing but ugliness and unhappiness.*

⁂

It's impossible to get along with someone who is always right

This is the French novelist Stendhal putting into words something we have surely all thought at some point or another. Before you say it to someone who seems to think they are always right, however, check out Mr Meagles under COUNT FIVE-AND-TWENTY, TATTYCORAM (see page 83) and learn from his mistakes.

It takes all the running you can do to stay in the same place

This is the Red Queen in Lewis Carroll's *Through the Looking-Glass,* and she says it after she has made Alice run faster and faster for quite a while; during this time, *The trees and the other things round them never changed their places at all: however fast they went, they never seemed to pass anything.* Alice, always rational and liking to get to the bottom of things, points out that in her country, *You'd generally get to somewhere else – if you ran very fast for a long time, as we've been doing.*

Not on the other side of the looking-glass, however: according to the Queen, not only does it take all the running you can do to stay in the same place, but *If you want to get somewhere else, you must run twice as fast as that.* It's the way many of us feel at the end of a hard week.

❖

The ladder of success is best climbed by stepping on the rungs of opportunity

The Greek god of opportunity, Caerus, is depicted with only one lock of hair, hanging down over his face: you have to grab him as he is coming towards you because once he has gone past it's too late – there's nothing to hold on to. This may have been the thought in the mind of Russian-American novelist Ayn Rand when she wrote these words: take your chances while you can.

The idea of being *ready* to grasp opportunities has been around for a long time. As Francis Bacon put it in 1605:

A man must make his opportunity, as oft as find it.

Or, to quote Oprah Winfrey nearly 400 years later:

Luck is preparation meeting opportunity.

So keep your eyes open and be prepared to clutch that forelock.

❧

The law is an ass

One of the most frequently misquoted of all quotations, this has its uses (in its abbreviated form) when the law *is* being an ass, but it's also rather fun in its original guise. Mr Bumble – the callous beadle of the workhouse in Dickens' *Oliver Twist* – has been accused of pawning jewellery belonging to Oliver's late mother and tries to blame the action on his wife:

> *'That is no excuse,' replied Mr Brownlow. 'You were present on the occasion of the destruction of these trinkets, and indeed are the more guilty of the two, in the eye of the law; for the law supposes that your wife acts under your direction.'*

> *'If the law supposes that,' said Mr Bumble, squeezing his hat emphatically in both hands, 'the law is a ass – a idiot. If that's the eye of the law, the law is a bachelor; and the worst I wish the law is, that his eye may be opened by experience.'*

It's rather a shame that *The law is a bachelor* isn't the expression that has caught on. It has a certain hen-pecked charm.

A liar needs a good memory

This is the cynical advice of the Roman rhetorician Quintilian, writing in the first century AD; it was echoed some 1,800 years later by the English novelist Samuel Butler, when he said:

> *Any fool can tell the truth, but it requires a man of some sense to lie well.*

... And another generation after that by the American-Canadian artist Farquhar Knowles, with:

> *There is nothing so pathetic as a forgetful liar.*

In other words, if you are going to maintain 'that's my story and I'm sticking to it', it's as well to have a firm grip on what your story is.

Others, less cynically, have extolled the virtue of tactful lying as a way of making the world go round: the twentieth-century Chinese philosopher Lin Yutang hit the nail on the head when he said:

> *Society can exist only on the basis that there is some amount of polished lying and that no one says exactly what he thinks.*

Imagine, for example, what would happen if everyone gave honest answers to questions such as 'Does my bum look big in this?'

Lord, **what fools these mortals be!**

The fairy Puck says this in Shakespeare's *A Midsummer Night's Dream,* laughing at the mess the four young (human) lovers have got themselves into. He's not being entirely fair, as a lot of the mess is his fault – he has cast a spell on the wrong person. But it's a useful expression for any time you think people around you are behaving foolishly, or if you are making an idiot of yourself, particularly in an affair of the heart.

The **more I see of people, the more I like dogs**

This line has been attributed to a number of people – most of them French and female, with minor variations in the wording. It appears in sundry French periodicals in the nineteenth century, but always with the suggestion that it is an established saying or that the writer is quoting someone else. So who said it first? Who knows? And it doesn't much matter – it's a useful line to come out with when someone (human) is misbehaving.

If you aren't a dog person, try the French novelist Colette:

> *Time spent with a cat is never wasted.*

And:

> *Our perfect companions never have fewer than four feet.*

It's clear from Colette's other writings that those perfect four-footed companions are, by definition, cats. And, because this entry seems to be entirely devoted to the French, see also page 37: WHOEVER WOULD BE CURED OF IGNORANCE MUST FIRST CONFESS IT.

No man is an island

Often misquoted, the rest of this line is *entire of itself* – meaning that no man (or woman, obviously) lives entirely separately from everyone else. The passage continues:

> *Every man is a piece of the continent, a part of the main . . . any man's death diminishes me, because I am involved in mankind, and therefore never send to know for whom the bells tolls; it tolls for thee.*

The tolling bell symbolizes death and this whole meditation, as it is called, is about the unitedness of humankind.

It's from the *Devotions* of John Donne, metaphysical poet, preacher and also author of some surprisingly frank (for a seventeenth-century churchman) love poems. His 'Elegy to His Mistress Going to Bed' includes lines that should probably be quoted only in the strictest privacy:

> *Licence my roving hands, and let them go*
> *Before, behind, between, above, below.*

If you ever hear anyone quoting *O my America! my new-found-land* as if it had something to do with America, you can put them right: it's the next line in this elegy and refers without a shadow of a doubt to what the poet's roving hands have found 'below'.

Although Donne clearly appreciates the female form, he doesn't demand perfection. In another elegy, called 'The Anagram', he praises the idea of loving a woman who isn't beautiful:

Love built on beauty, soon as beauty, dies . . .

. . . which is remarkably similar to the sentiment expressed a century later by the aristocratic Lady Mary Wortley Montagu:

A face is too slight a foundation for happiness.

See also page 152, WHEN HIS PISTOL MISSES FIRE, HE KNOCKS YOU DOWN WITH THE BUTT END OF IT, for the views of Oliver Goldsmith, a near-contemporary of Lady Mary, on the same subject.

❧

One half of the world cannot understand the pleasures of the other

Or, there's nowt so queer as folk and no accounting for taste. This is Jane Austen's Emma, expressing the same sentiment in a more genteel way. Her father (who worries about everything) is worrying about the rough play that his grandchildren seem to enjoy with their uncle and saying that he doesn't understand it. As Emma wisely points out, *That is the case with us all, Papa. One half of the world . . .* etc. Emma isn't right about much in the course of the book, but we can give her credit for this.

See also page 111, IN LITERATURE AS IN LOVE, WE ARE ASTONISHED AT WHAT IS CHOSEN BY OTHERS, for another take on the same theme.

Politeness is the art of selecting among one's real thoughts

Anne-Louise-Germaine Necker, more usually known as Madame de Staël, was renowned as the hostess of the foremost *salon* in Paris in the late eighteenth and early nineteenth centuries, except for periods she spent in exile because of her opposition to Napoleon: during those times she attracted the great thinkers of the day to her home in Switzerland instead. Having been accustomed since childhood to courtly life and good conversation – her father was director of finance to Louis XVI before the Revolution and her mother was another notable *salon* hostess – Madame de Staël had strong views on manners, as in the quotation above, and she was very dismissive of the etiquette that prevailed among the 'new nobility' of Napoleonic times:

> *Certainly there is nothing so difficult to learn, as the kind of politeness which is neither ceremonious nor familiar: it seems a trifle, but it requires a foundation in ourselves; for no one acquires it, if it is not inspired by early habits or elevation of mind.*

Her intelligence was much more than skin deep, however; her novels concern the limited freedom that women had in French society and the epigraph to one of them, *Delphine*, is taken from her own mother's writings:

> *A man must know how to stand out against public*
> *opinion, a woman how to submit to it.*

See also page 60, I would rather be a rebel than a slave, for other views on the role of women in society.

Poverty is no disgrace to a man, but it is confoundedly inconvenient

We met the Reverend Sydney Smith under I am glad I was not born before tea (see page 56), and here is another of his quotable remarks. He was full of them:

> *I think breakfasts so pleasant, because no one is*
> *conceited before one o'clock.*

And with reference to an unnamed dean who had clearly exasperated him:

> *[He] deserves to be preached to death by wild*
> *curates...*

... and on the historian Lord Macaulay:

> *He has occasional flashes of silence, that make his*
> *conversation perfectly delightful.*

This last remark pre-dates by some decades the composer Rossini's famous crack about Wagner, that he had *lovely moments, but awful quarter-hours,* but that in itself was a line that had been used before with reference to other artists not known for conciseness. The expression *mauvais quart d'heure* (French for 'bad quarter of an hour') was sufficiently well known in 1890s English society for Oscar Wilde to put it into his play *A Woman of No Importance*. In response to one character's remarking that *All life is very, very sad, is it not?*, another replies:

> *Life . . . is simply a* mauvais quart d'heure *made up of exquisite moments.*

Sydney Smith created more than his share of exquisite moments. Among them was the occasion when he was having dinner with a friend of whom he was fond but whose entire lack of sense of humour intrigued him. In the course of the meal Smith remarked of himself that:

> *. . . Though he was not generally considered an illiberal man, yet he must confess he had one little weakness, one secret wish, – he should like to roast a Quaker.*

Despite the fact that everyone else at the table was in hysterics, the humourless man could never – then or afterwards – be persuaded that this was a joke. With that in mind, the suggestion that you would like to roast a Quaker – or anyone else, for that matter – might be a fun thing to drop into the conversation with someone you particularly wish to outrage.

Reformers are always finally neglected, while the memoirs of the frivolous will always eagerly be read

These are the – perhaps rather self-serving – words of Chips Channon, American-born but British-based politician and socialite who, in the 1930s, '40s and '50s, wrote some of the most fascinating and frivolous diaries ever. While he could be discreet when he had to be, he was surely right when he said:

> *What is more dull than a discreet diary? One might just as well have a discreet soul.*

Others have felt the same way: the writer and critic Lytton Strachey, who as a member of the Bloomsbury Group had plenty to be indiscreet about, wrote:

> *Discretion is not the better part of biography.*

Oscar Wilde struck a more bitter note with:

> *Every great man nowadays has his disciples, and it is always Judas who writes the biography . . .*

. . . though you can't help feeling that Judas's version of the gospels would make interesting reading.

Something excellent and wholesome in its way, which was apt to become troublesome if you encouraged it overmuch

A description that on the face of it could be applied to almost anything, from beekeeping to yoga. In the original context it referred to the countryside: from a short story by Saki called 'The Music on the Hill', it was the attitude of a character who was *accustomed to nothing much more sylvan than 'leafy Kensington'* and who ended up finding the countryside very troublesome indeed. She would have sympathized with Sherlock Holmes' view:

> *The lowest and vilest alleys in London do not present a more dreadful record of sin than does the smiling and beautiful countryside.*

Or the eighteenth-century essayist William Hazlitt's:

> *There is nothing good to be had in the country, or if there is they will not let you have it.*

If you want a more positive take on the countryside, try the eighteenth-century poet John Dryden:

> *How blessed is he who leads a country life,*
> *Unvex'd with anxious cares and void of strife!*

Or Thoreau (LIVES OF QUIET DESPERATION, see page 90), who was very much in favour of the simple life:

> *While civilization has been improving our houses, it has not equally improved the men who are to inhabit them. It has created palaces, but it was not so easy to create noblemen and kings.*

Superstition is foolish, childish, primitive and irrational, but how much does it cost you to knock on wood?

Over the centuries, philosophers have tended to be anti superstition: in the seventeenth century Francis Bacon wrote that it *erecteth an absolute monarchy in the minds of men*, while in the eighteenth Edmund Burke called it *the religion of feeble minds*. But the American author Judith Viorst, in the words quoted above, takes a more pragmatic, twentieth-century view. Best known for her children's books, she has a great deal of worldly wisdom to offer adults, too:

> Being in love is better than being in jail, a dentist's chair or a holding pattern over Philadelphia, but not if he doesn't love you back.

And she offers an excellent analysis of sibling rivalry:

> If we are the younger, we may envy the older. If we are the older, we may feel that the younger is always being indulged. In other words, no matter what position we hold in family order of birth, we can prove beyond a doubt that we're being gypped.

❧

Three may keep a secret, if two of them are dead

According to the biblical Gospel of Matthew, Jesus, in the course of his Sermon on the Mount, advised, *Let not thy left hand know what thy right hand doeth*. He was talking about giving alms. Don't boast about your good deeds, was what he meant; they are their own reward. So the right hand not knowing what the left hand was doing was a good thing.

Nowadays, of course, we tend to use the expression as a sign of incompetence, as when one department in a company fails to communicate with another. If we want to talk about secrecy we are perhaps better off with the words quoted above, from Benjamin Franklin (WHAT

IS THE USE OF A NEW-BORN CHILD?, see page 179), or, going back even further, to Seneca in the first century AD:

> *If you wish another to keep your secret, first keep it to yourself.*

Not only can you not trust anyone, but, once the news is out, very little can be done about it. As White House Chief of Staff Bob Haldeman said with reference to the Watergate scandal:

> *Once the toothpaste is out of the tube, it is awfully hard to get it back in.*

❧

To see ourselves as others see us

This is what Hamlet might have called *a consummation devoutly to be wished* – seeing ourselves and our faults from other people's point of view. It is a line from Robert Burns' wonderfully titled poem 'To a Louse, On Seeing One on a Lady's Bonnet at Church' and in a translation from the original Scots it goes:

> *Oh, would some Power give us the gift*
> *To see ourselves as others see us!*
> *It would from many a blunder free us,*
> *And foolish notion:*
> *What airs in dress and gait would leave us,*
> *And even devotion!*

One interpretation is that the lady wouldn't have been so full of airs and graces if she'd known she had a louse on her bonnet.

What is true in the lamplight is not always true in the sunlight

A variation on the truism that things can look very different in the romantic glow of moonlight to how they appear 'in the cold light of dawn', these are the words of the eighteenth-century French moralist and critic Joseph Joubert. Joubert spent his life accumulating 'thoughts' on the human condition which were collected and published posthumously. He covered just about everything from the nature of God (*We always believe that God is like ourselves: the indulgent affirm him indulgent; the stern terrible*) to parenting (*In bringing up a child, think of its old age*). And, having lived through the French Revolution and the Napoleonic era, he came up with an observation that could have been written yesterday:

> *The age thought it was making progress in going over precipices.*

❦

You never can tell with ...

A. A. Milne's Winnie-the-Pooh said this a number of times – with references to bees, pawmarks and Heffalumps, to name but three. The bees might or might not have been suspicious of Pooh's motives – that was the thing you couldn't tell; the pawmarks might or might not have belonged to a Woozle; and Heffalumps may or may not come when you whistle. A useful expression, therefore, for almost any occasion when you can't tell what is going to happen.

3

YOUNG TOO SOON,
WISE TOO LATE

Among the subjects that have sparked people to the greatest eloquence are life's inevitable ups and downs. Here are their ideas on the highs and lows, the rough and the smooth.

❦

All hope abandon, ye who enter here

Often misquoted as 'Abandon hope, all ye who enter here', this is much more gloomy in the correct version: *every iota of hope*, every last scrap is to be abandoned. It's part of the inscription above the gate of Hell, through which the Italian poet Dante passes at the beginning of his epic poem *Divine Comedy*. Something to be said as you're waiting to go into the boss's office for an unpleasant meeting, perhaps.

❦

All that glisters is not gold

This is from Act II, scene vii of *The Merchant of Venice*, the scene in which the Prince of Morocco opens the gold casket.

Hang on. *The Merchant of Venice*? Isn't that Shylock and the pound of flesh? Well, yes, but this is a Shakespeare comedy – there has to be a ridiculous subplot. It has been decreed that wealthy Portia shall offer any suitor the opportunity to open one of three caskets, gold, silver or lead; one of them contains her portrait and she is to marry the man who finds it. We've already learned that the Prince of Morocco is pretty pleased with himself, so it's no surprise when he picks the gold casket, which bears the inscription *Who chooseth me shall gain what many men desire. Why, that's the lady*, he says, reasonably enough, and opens it, only to reveal a skull and a scroll with a verse beginning *All that glisters is not gold* and warning that *Gilded tombs do worms enfold*.

Don't judge a book by its glossy cover, it's saying, and Morocco departs discomfited.

An important thing to note here is that the word is *glisters*, not *glitters*. Pedants will pick you up on that every time. Extra points if you also know that the imagery recurs in Thomas Gray's 'Ode on the Death of a Favourite Cat':

> *Not all that tempts your wand'ring eyes*
> *And heedless hearts, is lawful prize;*
> *Nor all that glisters gold.*

The favourite cat has 'drowned in a tub of goldfishes' – another sad lesson on the vanity of seeking earthly rewards.

For more about Thomas Gray, see the next entry and, for more from *The Merchant of Venice*, see page 128: A DANIEL COME TO JUDGEMENT!

❧

As to posterity, I may ask . . . what has it ever done to oblige me?

Shades of Monty Python and *What did the Romans do for us?*, you might think, but in fact this is from a letter by the eighteenth-century poet Thomas Gray, best known for his 'Elegy in a Country Churchyard'. He's writing to a friend, explaining why he isn't doing any work at the moment: he's wandering round cathedrals and tombs and ruins, thinking. This may be, as he puts it, *to little purpose*, but who cares? Why should he worry about doing anything that posterity will consider worthwhile?

The ellipsis in the heading to this entry indicates the omission of the words *with some body whom I have forgot*, suggesting that Gray didn't make this witticism up, but is quoting . . . somebody. That somebody may well be Joseph Addison, the essayist and co-founder of *The Spectator* magazine, who had lived a generation or so earlier. Addison had written in 1714 (on the surprisingly modern subject of landowners managing their tree-planting sustainably):

> *I know when a Man talks of Posterity in Matters*
> *of this Nature, he is looked upon with an Eye of*
> *Ridicule by the cunning and selfish part of Mankind.*
> *Most People are of the Humour of an old Fellow of a*
> *College, who, when he was pressed by the Society to*

> *come into something that might redound to the good*
> *of their Successors, grew very peevish. We are always*
> *doing, says he, something for Posterity, but I would*
> *fain see Posterity do something for us.*

Whether Addison was genuinely quoting an elderly don or was making this up for the sake of a good story is open to speculation.

Avoiding danger is no safer in the long run than outright exposure . . .

. . . Life is either a daring adventure, or nothing.
So wrote Helen Keller, who in the early twentieth century earned fame by overcoming the handicaps of deafness and blindness to earn a degree and become an author and political activist. It's an idea that goes back a long way. The Roman historian Tacitus, writing in the first century AD, put it like this:

> *The desire for safety stands against every great and*
> *noble enterprise.*

While in the twentieth century the American politician James F. Byrnes said:

> *Too many people are thinking of security instead of*
> *opportunity. They seem more afraid of life than death.*

All persuasive ways of saying, 'Go for it!' when someone is erring too far on the side of caution.

Better by far you should forget and smile than that you should remember and be sad

Like many Victorians, Christina Rossetti spent a lot of her time pondering death and loss; these are the closing lines of her poem 'Remember', often read at funerals. She's hoping that, when she is dead, her loved ones will remember her, but not feel guilty when they find themselves moving on. In another poem she asks 'her dearest' not to sing sad songs for her; and in still another expresses pleasure that someone who didn't love her in life should be sorry for her when she dies young.

Not all of Rossetti's output is morbid: she must be one of the few Victorians to work a wombat into a poem. But there he is, in 'Goblin Market', in a passage describing the various goblin merchants encountered on the road:

> *One had a cat's face,*
> *One whisk'd a tail,*
> *One tramp'd at a rat's pace,*
> *One crawl'd like a snail,*
> *One like a wombat prowl'd obtuse and furry,*
> *One like a ratel tumbled hurry skurry.*

Obtuse and furry is so beautifully accurate that you can't help feeling she must have seen a wombat – but where? She lived quite close to the newly opened Regent's Park Zoo and is known to have visited it, but did they have a wombat in the 1850s? The imagination could waste a lot of time on this quite unimportant question.

To return to the point, lest you wonder where Robert Galbraith (a.k.a. J. K. Rowling) found the title for the first Cormoran Strike novel, that is Christina Rossetti too, back to less cheerful mode:

Why were you born when the snow was falling?
You should have come to the cuckoo's calling.

A bit tough to blame someone for the season of their birthday, but that poem is called 'A Dirge' and is really bemoaning the person's death (which also, inevitably, happened at the wrong time of year).

❦

Count five-and-twenty, Tattycoram

Possibly the most annoying remark in all of Dickens and one that is bound to irritate anyone you say it to. Tattycoram is a character in *Little Dorrit*; a foundling who has been taken in by the kindly Meagles family, she is regarded by them as sullen, passionate and subject to violent tempers. Mr Meagles is forever telling her to *count five-and-twenty* before flying off the handle – and you don't have to read the book to guess how well that goes down. Tattycoram would have sympathized with the drunken Katherine in David Hare's play *The Secret Rapture* and her experience of Alcoholics Anonymous meetings:

When you get angry they tell you to count to five before you reply. Why should I count to five? It's what happens before you count to five which makes life interesting.

❦

A fool at forty is a fool indeed

This was said by the eighteenth-century English poet Edward Young, in a collection of satires called *Love of Fame: the Universal Passion*; he expanded on the thought in his long poem *The Complaint: or Night Thoughts on Life, Death, and Immortality*:

> *At thirty man suspects himself a fool,*
> *Knows it at forty, and reforms his plan;*
> *At fifty chides his infamous delay,*
> *Pushes his prudent purpose to resolve;*
> *In all the magnanimity of thought*
> *Resolves, and re-resolves, then dies the same.*

The idea that there is no fool like an old fool was already well established in 1546, when the writer John Heywood included it in a collection of proverbs. But in the twentieth century the American judge Jacob M. Braude gave us a new twist:

> *There's no fool like an old fool – you can't beat experience.*

Braude seems to have spent many of his off-duty hours coining aphorisms and publishing them in books aimed at speakers and writers; among those worth adding to your collection are:

> *Life is a grindstone: whether it grinds you down or polishes you up depends on what you're made of.*

> *Consider how hard it is to change yourself and you'll understand what little chance you have in trying to change others.*

And:

> *There is no way to catch a snake that is as safe as not catching him …*

… though it is difficult to imagine a genuine set of circumstances that would allow you to work that last one into the conversation.

❦

For all sad words of tongue or pen …

… The saddest are these: 'It might have been'.
Lots of wise words have been written lamenting things that we haven't done rather than things that we have: the American journalist Sydney J. Harris wrote that:

> *Regret for the things we did can be tempered by time; it is regret for the things we did not do that is inconsolable.*

The academic Deborah Tannen expresses a similar sentiment as:

> *We all feel wistfulness or regret about roads not taken.*

But the words quoted above – written by the American poet John Greenleaf Whittier – are among the most poignant on the theme. They're from a poem called 'Maud Muller', in which a judge, influenced by money and ambition, doesn't marry the country lass he loves. Both live unhappily ever after – she in poverty, he in a gilded cage. 'Follow your heart' is surely the lesson here.

If you can keep your head . . .

. . . when all about you
Are losing theirs and blaming it on you . . .
These are the opening lines of Kipling's 'If', once voted the UK's favourite poem. Two more lines are inscribed above the entrance through which players pass on their way on to Centre Court at Wimbledon:

> *If you can meet with triumph and disaster*
> *And treat those two impostors just the same . . .*

The poem continues with various other sets of character-building circumstances which you might have to face in the course of life – dreaming, but not making dreams your master, being lied about but not dealing in lies, that sort of thing. It's all one very long sentence and it ends with *You'll be a Man, my son!*

Note the capital M, and the gender-specificness: this was about the qualities that, for better or for worse (and Kipling would have said very much for better), made the British Empire-builder what he was. But the attitude doesn't have to be imperialist. About a generation later and on the other side of the Atlantic, the novelist Willa Cather was writing, in a letter to her mother, a similar sentiment with a more feminine slant:

> *When will we be strongminded enough to treat*
> *compliments as carelessly as we do insults, and live our*
> *lives as we want to, letting nothing interfere?*

You can't help feeling that, if she was able to treat insults carelessly, she was impressively strongminded already.

In a real dark night of the soul, it is always three o'clock in the morning

There's quite a lot of gloom in F. Scott Fitzgerald, and this is him at his gloomiest. It comes in an essay called 'The Crack-Up', written in 1936 when he was forty, suffering from depression and aware that his greatest works and the height of his fame were in the past – he described himself as having *cracked like an old plate*. To put the line in context, he writes that *the standard cure* for someone in his condition is *to consider those in actual destitution or physical suffering*:

> *This is an all-weather beatitude for gloom in general and fairly salutary daytime advice for everyone. But at three o'clock in the morning, a forgotten package has the same tragic importance as a death sentence, and the cure doesn't work – and in a real dark night of the soul it is always three o'clock in the morning, day after day.*

It didn't get any better for Fitzgerald: he was dead within four years. But it's a brilliant description of misery and despair.

❦

It is the bright day that brings forth the adder . . .

. . . And that craves wary walking.

So reasons Marcus Brutus, in Shakespeare's *Julius Caesar*, as he is persuading himself that Caesar must be assassinated. If Caesar accepts the crown that the Roman people have offered him, it may change his nature: the 'bright day' that represents kingship may bring out the worst in him. In the play, this conclusion is effectively Caesar's death warrant – once Brutus is on side, the conspirators are ready to roll. In modern life it's a rather pessimistic warning against judging by (good) appearances – or perhaps against going out on a sunny day without your shoes on.

See also page 43: *ALEA IACTA EST*.

It's but little good you'll do a-watering the last year's crop

These words are spoken by Mrs Poyser, a neighbour of the Bede family, in George Eliot's novel *Adam Bede* (1859). Adam's drunken father has just died and Mrs Poyser is encouraging the widow to *keep up her heart*. Not a tactful woman, she observes that it would be better if we were appreciative of people while they were still alive, rather than after they've gone; she concludes her bracing speech with the words given above. Mr Poyser, *feeling that his wife's words were, as usual, rather incisive than soothing*, hastily changes the subject – you get the impression he has done that quite a lot in the course of his married life.

Nevertheless, if you want a particularly uncomforting variation on 'Don't close the stable door after the horse has bolted' or 'It's no use crying over spilt milk', this could come in handy.

I've learned that even when I have pains, I don't have to be one

This is poet and novelist Maya Angelou, setting an example to all the moaners and whiners of this world. Goodness knows, as a child victim of both rape and racism, she could have done her share of moaning if she wanted, but she had an extraordinary ability to focus on the positive and the uplifting. It's perhaps best summarized in this line:

> *Life is not measured by the number of breaths you take but by the moments that take your breath away.*

You can't argue with that. Nor can you argue with another great black female writer, Toni Morrison, on a similar theme:

> *If you want to fly, you have to give up the things that weigh you down.*

Like Angelou, Morrison has wise things to say on the subject of race and racism:

> *If you can only be tall if someone else is on their knees, then you have a serious problem.*

Angelou and Morrison both write a lot about the black woman's position in society; so, too, does Alice Walker. It's worth pausing to think about:

> *The animals of the world exist for their own reasons. They were not made for humans any more than black people were made for white, or women created for men.*

And:

> *The most common way people give up their power is by thinking they don't have any.*

In apartheid South Africa in 1976, the activist Steve Biko was saying much the same thing:

> *The most potent weapon in the hands of the oppressor is the mind of the oppressed.*

Like asking Dracula if he had blood

A line from Pat Barker's novel *Noonday*. One character offers another a drink and he replies, 'Whisky, if you've got it.' We already know the drinking habits of the host, so the unspoken comment, *If he'd got it. Like asking Dracula if he had blood,* is precisely what we'd have thought ourselves if we'd been quick enough. A useful alternative to 'Is the Pope a Catholic?' when the obvious is being asked or stated.

Lives of quiet desperation

According to Thoreau (BEWARE OF ALL ENTERPRISES THAT REQUIRE NEW CLOTHES, see page 47), this is what 'the mass of men' lead. In 1845, Thoreau built himself a cabin on the shore of Walden Pond in Concord, Massachusetts, and lived there alone, 'a mile from any neighbour', for over two years. He wrote a book, *Walden*, about his experiences, and it is in its early pages that he comes up with this maxim, having been talking about how most people have to work so hard to keep body and soul together that they have no time for the finer things of life. He's advising people to make more choices, not to follow in the footsteps of their seniors just for the sake of it, not to assume that they need what are in fact luxuries, not to think they are enriching their souls when all they are doing is making money. He's aiming for self-sufficiency, but he also has a rebellious streak; you might also like to quote:

> *If I repent of anything, it is very likely to be my good behaviour. What demon possessed me that I behaved so well?*

Many thinkers and composers of maxims have maintained that we regret things we haven't done rather than things we've done (see page 85: FOR ALL SAD WORDS OF TONGUE OR PEN); Thoreau is perhaps the only one who openly regrets behaving well.

❧

Merely corroborative detail, intended to give artistic verisimilitude to an otherwise bald and unconvincing narrative

From Gilbert and Sullivan's *The Mikado*, these are words spoken by Pooh-Bah, the ridiculous civil servant designated 'Lord High Everything Else' (everything apart from Lord High Executioner, that is). He and two other characters have been describing to the Mikado an execution they say has taken place earlier in the day. It's a lie, but it pleases the Mikado, so Pooh-Bah has embellished the story with minutiae about the severed head bowing to him with the deference due to a man of pedigree – and the words given above are his justification for this flight of fancy. Unfortunately, the man they claim to have beheaded turns out to be the Mikado's son and heir, which rather complicates the situation.

It's all nonsense, of course, but a number of people come close to being put to death before things are sorted out. It's not hugely likely that you'll ever find yourself in a comparable situation – and chances are you'll be worried about more important things than corroborative detail if you are – but the expression can be adapted to suit any mildly fanciful or long-winded story.

Pooh-Bah, incidentally, has found his way into dictionaries, defined as *a pompous, self-important official holding several offices at once and fulfilling none of them*. You may well know – or have read in the media about – someone to whom that description could usefully be applied.

My salad days, when I was green in judgement

We tend just to say 'my salad days', without further elaboration, but you may feel that the extended version has more gravitas. It's from Shakespeare's *Antony and Cleopatra*, and the speaker is Cleopatra herself, referring to a time when she was younger and more naïve. In fact she's talking about the time when she thought she was in love with Julius Caesar and comparing it unfavourably to the present, when she *knows* she's in love with Antony. She's wiser now. (This is in Act I. By the end of Act IV she's holding an asp to her breast. Draw what conclusions you will.)

Over the years, the nuance of the expression has changed somewhat – one's salad days tend to be a time of youthful carefreeness rather than foolish and regrettable inexperience; the 1950s musical *Salad Days* is about the joys of being young and frivolous.

Shakespeare's is, by the way, an early use of the word *green* to mean naïve and easily fooled. The OED's first citation is dated 1605 and *Antony and Cleopatra* was first performed in about 1607.

❀

Nothing is so good as it seems beforehand

In context, this is a particularly sad line, from George Eliot's *Silas Marner*. The wealthy but childless Nancy discovers that when she married her husband Godfrey he was a widower with a daughter and had treated his late wife badly. This opens her eyes to the weakness of his character, which is unfortunate enough; but the true sorrow is that, if only she'd known, she would have adopted the little girl and had the joy of having a child to love. The thing that isn't as good as it seemed beforehand is her marriage.

Out of context, the quotation is a useful way of spreading gloom and doom whenever this seems the right thing to do.

That well-known gloom-spreader Dorothy Parker, whom you won't often find being quoted in the same breath as George Eliot, shared her views on this subject:

> *The only dependable law of life – everything is always worse than you thought it was going to be.*

For more from Dorothy Parker, see page 101: WHEREVER SHE WENT, INCLUDING HERE, IT WAS AGAINST HER BETTER JUDGEMENT.

❦

O, that this too too solid flesh would melt

From Shakespeare's *Hamlet* – his first major soliloquy in the play. Hamlet has just learned that his father was murdered by his uncle, Claudius, and has to put a brave face on the fact that, only two months later, Claudius has married Hamlet's mother, Gertrude. She has just urged Hamlet to stop mourning his father and to treat Claudius as a loved and loving replacement. It's all too much for Hamlet and he wishes he could die. Suicide is a sin, so the alternative desire is for his flesh simply to melt away. As with the murder in *Macbeth* (THERE'S HUSBANDRY IN HEAVEN, see page 178), you don't have to be contemplating death to use this expression. You could just be embarking on a diet that is going to make your life a misery for a while.

❦

One slow descent into respectability

A variation on the theme of growing old disgracefully, this is the way the model Mandy Rice-Davies described her life after she had been involved in the huge 1960s political and sexual scandal of the Profumo Affair at the age of eighteen. After that, almost anything that happened was going to be an anti-climax.

Mandy Rice-Davies always had a way about her – she is the one who, when told in court that a prominent peer had denied having an affair with her, said matter-of-factly, *Well, he would, wouldn't he?*

Our revels now are ended

Or, as the publicans say, 'Time, ladies and gentlemen, please!' This comes towards the end of Shakespeare's *The Tempest*, when the magician Prospero is preparing to abandon his powers and leave the enchanted island on which he has been living. He's about to return to the real world, where he is – of all unmagical things – the rightful Duke of Milan. The party's over, in other words; it's time to go home.

Pathetic. That's what it is. Pathetic

So says Eeyore, A. A. Milne's gloomy donkey in *Winnie-the-Pooh*, when everyone seems to have forgotten his birthday. 'Eeyorish' has passed into the language as a rather self-consciously cute way of saying 'miserable, down in the dumps', just as 'Tiggerish' (after the character introduced in Milne's sequel, *The House at Pooh Corner*) means bouncy and optimistic. But if you can say 'pathetic' as if you were spitting rather than talking, you can vent a lot of spleen. Eeyore certainly did.

Something is rotten in the state of Denmark

Hamlet again; this is said early in the play by Marcellus, one of the officers guarding the castle of Elsinore, just after the appearance of the Ghost of Hamlet's father. The Ghost has lured his son out of earshot so that he can explain that he has been murdered and exhort Hamlet to avenge him; Hamlet's companions are left flummoxed and apprehensive. So Marcellus's remark is a serious one, but if you use it out of context you can apply it to a variety of situations, from discovering something in the fridge that is malodorously past its sell-by date to finding out about a nasty piece of office politics.

That miserable No-Man's Land between Meccano and Sex

This is the great English humorist Alan Coren on the subject of adolescence or, more specifically, being fourteen and *wide open to suggestions that life was hell*. Part of what made life hell was being:

> *... suddenly aware of how tall girls were, and of*
> *how poorly a box of dead butterflies and a luminous*
> *compass fit a man for a smooth initiation into the*
> *perfumed garden.*

Coren isn't by any means the only person to have recorded troubles in adolescence. Slightly coarser – and omitting the casual allusion to fifteenth-century Arabic erotica – is the attitude of literature's greatest dysfunctional teenager, Holden Caulfield in J. D. Salinger's novel *The Catcher in the Rye*:

> *That's the thing about girls. Every time they do*
> *something pretty, even if they're not much to look at, or*
> *even if they're sort of stupid, you fall half in love with*
> *them, and then you never know where the hell you*
> *are. Girls. Jesus Christ. They can drive you crazy. They*
> *really can.*

For a female perspective, Nell in Margaret Atwood's story 'My Last Duchess' describes the horrors of the early stages of the dating ritual, including *the breathy fumbling around in parked cars ... the war of zippers and buttons,* until in due course a stalemate is reached:

> *Neither side would know what was supposed to come*
> *next. To go forward was unthinkable, to go back*
> *impossible.*

Both Holden and Nell might have derived comfort from a remark made by the American journalist Earl Wilson:

> *Snow and adolescence are the only problems that*
> *disappear if you ignore them long enough.*

See also page 99: AN UNANSWERABLE COMBINATION OF INNOCENCE AND INSOLENCE.

There is no greater sorrow than to recall a time of happiness in misery

The fourteenth-century Italian poet Dante wrote this in his *Inferno*, but he was echoing the Roman philosopher and politician Boethius from a thousand years earlier: *In all adversity of fortune, the unhappiest of misfortunes is to have been happy.*

You may feel this is a somewhat negative attitude. The optimist, or even the pragmatist, may prefer to burst into song at this point, remembering two great singers of the twentieth century. Frank Sinatra, doing it His Way, famously sang about having regrets that were too few to mention, while Edith Piaf boasted throbbingly that she regretted nothing at all.

See also page 78: ALL HOPE ABANDON, YE WHO ENTER HERE.

Tomorrow is another day

Made famous by Scarlett O'Hara at the end of *Gone with the Wind*, this line is much older than that: it was being used as a maxim a hundred years before Margaret Mitchell's novel was published in 1936. It isn't about procrastination (for that, see page 61: IF IT WEREN'T FOR THE LAST MINUTE, NOTHING WOULD GET DONE);

rather, it refers to the blank canvas, the new opportunities that tomorrow presents. Just remember, however, before you tread blindly down an optimistic path, that someone else involved may, frankly, not give a damn.

❧

An unanswerable combination of innocence and insolence

This is the twentieth-century novelist Alice Thomas Ellis's description of adolescence. It appears in her *The Skeleton in the Cupboard* and goes on to elaborate on the *curious superiority* with which teenagers respond to being lectured on society's demands:

> *It is unlikely that they have yet done anything truly dreadful and they suspect that their elders probably have. To be told how to behave by a person steeped in moral turpitude is annoying to everyone, but more particularly to the young.*

Too much to quote at any given moment, perhaps, but plenty to strike a chord with any parent or teacher of teenagers.

❧

We were young, we were merry, we were very very wise

This is the opening line of 'Unwelcome' by Mary Elizabeth Coleridge, a great-great niece of the more famous Samuel Taylor Coleridge. It's actually a Gothic poem about unwelcome presences – ghosts? – at a feast, but taken out of context it becomes a rather jolly way of reflecting on the know-it-all attitude of our younger selves (see also pages 99 and 102: AN UNANSWERABLE COMBINATION OF INNOCENCE AND INSOLENCE and YOUNG TOO SOON, WISE TOO LATE).

The weather is like the Government, always in the wrong

In 1758, in the magazine *The Idler*, Dr Samuel Johnson, the great lexicographer, wrote:

> *When two Englishmen meet, their first talk is of the weather . . .*

. . . an observation that remains true to this day, unless there's a big football match on. Over a century later, Jerome K. Jerome, best known as the author of *Three Men in a Boat*, produced a collection of essays called *Idle Thoughts of an Idle Fellow* and it's from this that the above words are taken. Jerome's idle thoughts cover subjects as wide-ranging as memory, babies and getting on in the world (*If you are foolish enough to be contented, don't show it, but grumble with the rest*), but it is on the weather that he resonates most, at least with British readers. After describing the way we complain about the seasons:

> *In summer time we say it is stifling; in winter that it is killing; in spring and autumn we find fault with it for being neither one thing nor the other, and wish it would make up its mind . . .*

. . . he reaches the conclusion:

> *We shall never be content until each man makes his own weather, and keeps it to himself. If that cannot be arranged, we would rather do without it altogether.*

This was in 1886, before anyone had heard a whisper of global warming. It's good to know that the national passion for the subject has such a long and prestigious pedigree.

❧

Wherever she went, including here, it was against her better judgement

The American wit, essayist and poet Dorothy Parker thought this might be a good thing to have on her tombstone. It wasn't her only possible epitaph: the plaque on her grave mentions that she suggested *Excuse my dust*; on another occasion she's said to have proposed *This is on me*. But given that she had two failed marriages (three if you count the fact that she married the same man twice and separated from him twice) and many unhappy love affairs, the idea that she seemed always to be acting against her better judgement is perhaps the most appropriate of all.

It's impossible to leave it at that with Dorothy Parker: she had so many wonderful things to say. Just two more: *The first thing I do in the morning is clean my teeth and sharpen my tongue* and – surprising gentle and wise for a woman known for her acidity – *Never throw mud: you can miss the target but your hands will remain dirty.*

And, on the subject of second marriages, Dr Johnson, on hearing that a man who had been unhappy with his first wife had married again soon after her death, described this as *the triumph of hope over experience*. What he would have said about Dorothy Parker's errors of judgement is anyone's guess.

❧

Young too soon, wise too late

Another subject on which the philosophers seem to agree. This is Benjamin Franklin; George Bernard Shaw is often quoted as saying:

> *Youth is wasted on the young.*

Or perhaps:

> *Youth is the most beautiful thing in this world – and what a pity that it has to be wasted on children!*

He may never have said this at all, but it's so widely quoted and so completely in character that it's hard to believe he didn't. Lord Asquith, British Prime Minister in the early twentieth century, did say:

> *Youth would be an ideal state if it came a little later in life …*

… while the sixteenth-century French scholar Henri Estienne wrote something that is usually translated as:

> *If youth but knew; if old age but could.*

A later French wit, Georges Courteline, took a more pragmatic line:

It is better to waste one's youth than to do nothing with it at all.

And yet another Frenchman, Antoine de Saint-Exupéry, saw it from the point of view of the young:

Grown-ups never understand anything for themselves and it is tiresome for children to be always and forever explaining things to them.

Decide on your standpoint, admit (if only to yourself) how old you are and you are likely to find something useful in that lot.

4

GOODNESS HAD NOTHING
TO DO WITH IT

Love, sex, friendship, hatred – here is what the famous and the infamous have had to say on human relationships in all their colours.

❖

Being an old maid is like death by drowning, a really delightful sensation after you cease to struggle

A comforting thought for the unattached among us, from Edna Ferber, the Pulitzer Prize-winning novelist who wrote, among many other things, the books on which the musical *Show Boat* and the James Dean film *Giant* were based. She lived to the age of eighty-two without ever, apparently, engaging in a romantic relationship of any kind, so presumably she knew what she was talking about when it came to being an 'old maid'. What experience she had of drowning is less easy to assess.

❖

Being jealous of a beautiful woman is not going to make you more beautiful

Married nine times, the (very beautiful) Hungarian actress Zsa Zsa Gabor had plenty to say on love, looks, marriage and divorce. In addition to the words quoted above, she said, looking back on her own chequered career:

> I am a marvellous housekeeper. Every time I leave a man, I keep his house.

> I never hated a man enough to give him his diamonds back.

> If you like a man and he likes you, you should get married as fast as you can. Otherwise you are both going to change your minds. There's plenty of time for that after marriage.

And, if she wasn't always consistent, she had an answer for that, too:

> Love is not logical and consistent. So why should my advice be? If you want that kind of thinking, go to a computer. Computers are always logical and consistent, and you see how often they get proposed to.

A Book of Verses underneath the Bough ...

... *A Jug of Wine, a Loaf of Bread – and Thou.*
Most people quoting these lines stop there, but that is to distort the sense. The verse goes on:

> *[Thou] beside me singing in the wilderness –*
> *Oh, Wilderness were Paradise enow!*

So it isn't just thy presence that turns the Wilderness into Paradise, it's thy singing, too. A small thing, but to lovers with no ear for music, it might make all the difference.

These words are from Edward Fitzgerald's nineteenth-century translation of *The Rubaiyat of Omar Khayyam*. *Rubaiyat* is a traditional Persian verse form and Omar Khayyam was a Persian poet and astronomer who lived in the eleventh and twelfth centuries. You can debate (endlessly) the philosophy behind the poems and whether or not Omar wrote all of them, but most people don't bother and just quote these few lines because they sound romantic.

Fitzgerald and Omar between them also came up with a quatrain of which Horace would have approved (No POEMS CAN LIVE LONG OR PLEASE THAT ARE WRITTEN BY WATER-DRINKERS, see page 173):

> *Ah, fill the cup – what boots it to repeat*
> *How time is slipping underneath our feet:*
> *Unborn to-morrow, and dead yesterday,*
> *Why fret about them if to-day be sweet?*

But that was in another country ...

... And besides, the wench is dead.
You *could* use this remark to encourage someone to move on from something that no longer matters. But not, really

not, if there is any chance that they will recognize the source.

It comes from Christopher Marlowe's play *The Jew of Malta*, written about 1590. Two Christian friars are accusing Barabas, the wealthy Jew of the title, of various crimes: he freely confesses to usury and the words quoted above are his dismissive, shoulder-shrugging admission of fornication. It's not an exhortation to let go of the past; it is a hideously, jaw-droppingly callous way of saying, 'Oh, come on. Who cares?'

The critic Sheridan Morley, reviewing a 1999 revival of this play, observed that it was seldom produced, *not least because it has something to offend just about everyone.* Since it includes Barabas poisoning a convent of nuns with a vat of rice pudding, he could well have been right.

The Wench is Dead is also the title of a Colin Dexter novel (and later TV adaptation) in which Inspector Morse, bored rigid in hospital, sets himself the task of solving a murder that took place over a century earlier. The point there, too, is that nobody understands why he is bothering. More 'let sleeping dogs lie' than anything more positive.

Chumps always make the best husbands . . .

. . . All unhappy marriages come from the husbands having brains.

So wrote the comic genius P. G. Wodehouse, who was married, apparently happily, to the same woman for over sixty years. It's tempting to ponder if he is drawing on first-hand experience here.

Wodehouse's novels are full of chumps, married and unmarried. But their family relationships are rarely conventional. The parentless, sibling-less Bertie Wooster, frequently a fiancé but never a groom, is nevertheless beset by aunts:

> It is no use telling me that there are bad aunts and good aunts. At the core, they are all alike. Sooner or later, out pops the cloven hoof.

Something to throw into the conversation, perhaps, when your own relatives are getting you down.

Goodness had nothing to do with it

The actress Mae West was known for her curvaceous figure, clinging dresses and unashamed sexual provocativeness. She spoke these words in 1932 in her first film, *Night After Night*, after the hat-check girl at a night club exclaimed, *Goodness! What beautiful diamonds!* It was a small role in an otherwise forgotten movie, but the line launched West's career and made her co-star George Raft, already an established actor, vow never to work with her again: *She stole everything but the cameras*, he said. *She had me licked.*

It remains a good response any time anyone makes a mindless remark beginning, 'Goodness!' Particularly if you can do the husky, innuendo-laden voice.

He jests at scars that never felt a wound

Romeo says this just before he eavesdrops on Juliet on her balcony (A ROSE BY ANY OTHER NAME, see page 30); his friends have been teasing him about falling in love and he basically means, 'It's all right for them, they don't know what it's like.' So this is a posh way of saying just that.

❦

I think this is the beginning of a beautiful friendship

Casablanca is, of course, the film in which no one says, in so many words, *Play it again, Sam*. But many of the things they do say are so quotable that this hardly matters. The line given above is the last in the film, spoken by Humphrey Bogart's character Rick as he and the French policeman Captain Renault disappear into the mist. The former has always maintained *I stick my neck out for nobody*; the latter calls himself a *poor corrupt official*, but between them they have nobly allowed the Resistance leader and his wife (Ingrid Bergman, whom Rick loves) to escape to America – this is where the speech about *The problems of three little people don't amount to a hill of beans in this crazy world* comes in. Rick has also shot the local Nazi leader, Renault has covered it up (by instructing his men to *Round up the usual suspects*) and the two are now going to leave Casablanca together to join the Free French in another part of Africa. They both have more heart than they would have had us believe.

Two more before we let the credits roll: the womanizing Renault, overhearing Rick refusing to make a date with a girlfriend, says disapprovingly:

> *How extravagant you are, throwing away women like*
> *that. Someday they may be scarce.*

He also asks Rick how he ended up in Casablanca, of all benighted places:

> *My health. I came to Casablanca for the waters.*
> *The waters? What waters? We're in the desert.*
> *I was misinformed.*

A useful brush-off if someone argues you into a corner.

If Cleopatra's nose had been shorter, the whole history of the world would have been different

The most frequently quoted remark of the seventeenth-century French philosopher Blaise Pascal. If you've heard this before and wondered what it meant, here are the lines that precede it:

> *Whoever will know fully the vanity of man has but to*
> *consider the causes and the effects of love. The cause is*
> *an unknown quantity, and the effects are terrible. This*
> *unknown quantity, so small a matter that we cannot*
> *recognize it, moves a whole country, princes, armies,*
> *and all the world.*

In other words, such a trivial matter as an alteration in the size of Cleopatra's nose might have stopped Antony falling in love with her and dragging the Roman Republic into civil war. If that hadn't happened, the Republic might never have turned into the Empire and the Romans might not have taken over significant chunks of the known world. And we'd never have had to debate what the Romans did for us, because they wouldn't have done anything.

Where that English translation uses *unknown quantity*, Pascal wrote *je ne sais quoi*, an expression he rightly attributes to his contemporary, the playwright Pierre Corneille, who had coined it in his play *Rodogune* twenty years earlier. Corneille, too, is referring to love – he writes about:

> ... *mismatched souls who become attached to each other and let themselves be stung by those* je ne sais quoi *that one can't explain.*

It sounds better in French and in verse, but it's a good example of the randomness of falling in love. Not only that, but you'll impress people by knowing that this well-known idiom originated in a minor work by a playwright who is today barely remembered outside a French classroom.

❧

In literature as in love, we are astonished at what is chosen by others

If you want a flash way to say, 'There's no accounting for taste', try this quote from the French novelist and biographer André Maurois. And if anyone asks you who he might be, reply that he is also the man who said:

> *If men could regard the events of their lives with more open minds they would frequently discover that they did not really desire the thing they failed to obtain.*

It may not answer the question, but it will give you a moment to regroup while they think about it.

Love is not love which alters when it alteration finds

A glowing tribute to the steadfastness of true love, this is from Shakespeare's sonnet 116. It goes on to say:

> *O no; it is an ever-fixed mark*
> *That looks on tempests, and is never shaken.*

Love survives, in other words, whatever is thrown at it and even when age has taken its toll. Just a little bit unrealistic? Or very sweet? Your call.

For more on love from a Shakespearean sonnet, see page 117: SHALL I COMPARE THEE TO A SUMMER'S DAY?

Love is the delusion that one woman differs from another

Among the many accomplishments of the satirist H. L. Mencken was that he was an expert on American English. In the course of his career he put together two *Mencken Chrestomathies* – collections designed to help students of the language. As the first of these contained both the definition given above and:

> *Puritanism. The haunting fear that someone,*
> *somewhere, may be happy . . .*

... it's interesting to speculate on just how useful they can have been to any foreigner making a serious effort to learn English.

Mencken had a lofty contempt for his fellow human being. The following gibe is often quoted in a shorter form, but to get the full impact of the sarcasm you need the whole thing:

> *No one in this world, so far as I know – and I have searched the records for years, and employed agents to help me – has ever lost money by underestimating the intelligence of the great masses of the plain people.*

See also page 155, THE BALLOT IS STRONGER THAN THE BULLET, for Mencken's views on democracy.

Love looks not with the eyes but with the mind...

... and therefore is wing'd Cupid painted blind.
This is Helena in Shakespeare's *A Midsummer Night's Dream*, bemoaning the fact that Demetrius doesn't love her, even though she is reckoned to be as beautiful as the woman he does love. Love can also make us do some foolish things, seeing qualities in the loved one that simply aren't there:

> *Things base and vile, holding no quantity,*
> *Love can transpose to form and dignity.*

In Helena's case, the fairies Puck and Oberon intervene and all ends happily; in real life, you might find another line from *A Midsummer Night's Dream* appropriate:

> *The course of true love never did run smooth.*

❦

The maximum of temptation with the maximum of opportunity

This combination is how the playwright George Bernard Shaw explained the popularity of marriage. He was obviously talking about sexual opportunities; Robert Louis Stevenson took a more pessimistic view. In his collection of essays *Virginibus Puerisque* ('For Girls and Boys'), he wrote:

> *Marriage is like life in this – that it is a field of battle, and not a bed of roses.*

> *Marriage is a step so grave and decisive that it attracts light-headed, variable men by its very awfulness.*

And, most gloomily of all:

> *To marry is to domesticate the Recording Angel. Once you are married, there is nothing left for you, not even suicide, but to be good.*

It's odd to observe that, although Shaw was married to the same woman – a fellow political activist named Charlotte Payne-Townshend – for forty-five years, it is widely believed that the marriage was never consummated: he seems not to have availed himself of that maximum of opportunity. Stevenson, on the other hand, seems to have been devoted to his wife and she to him: where did he get all that cynicism from? It just makes you wonder.

See page 45, ALL BEGINNINGS ARE DELIGHTFUL; THE THRESHOLD IS THE PLACE TO PAUSE, for another attitude to marriage.

Never in this world can hatred by stilled by hatred . . .

. . . it will be stilled only by non-hatred.
This is a pronouncement of Buddha's in the fifth or sixth century BC, but you can imagine that lots of people have expressed opinions on the subject of hatred. To turn to another religion, the Litany in the Anglican Book of Common Prayer contains a formidable list of things from which it asks the Lord to spare us, including *envy, hatred, and malice, and all uncharitableness.*

The American poet and novelist Maya Angelou (I'VE LEARNED THAT EVEN WHEN I HAVE PAINS, I DON'T HAVE TO BE ONE, see page 89) put it neatly when she said:

> *Hate, it has caused a lot of problems in the world, but has not solved one yet.*

And Nelson Mandela, in his autobiography *Long Walk to Freedom*, struck an inspiring note:

> *No one is born hating another person because of the colour of his skin, or his background, or his religion. People must learn to hate, and if they can learn to hate, they can be taught to love.*

Let's hope so, because although there are those who will maintain (quoting *Hamlet*) that they must be cruel only to be kind, no one has a good word to say about hatred. Ursula Le Guin put the two neatly together in her story 'The Stars Below':

> *No granite is so hard as hatred and no clay so cold as cruelty.*

Both of them best avoided, whether you are a follower of Buddha, Le Guin or the Book of Common Prayer.

❀

Oh gracious, why wasn't I born old and ugly?

So wonders Miss Miggs, an unappealing character in Dickens' *Barnaby Rudge*; she is a jailor at Newgate Prison and is provoked into making the remark by the unwanted attentions of the hangman, Mr Dennis. She over-rates her own attractions, though: we have been told that she is *slender and shrewish, of a rather uncomfortable figure, and though not absolutely ill-looking, of a sharp and acid visage.* We also know her views on the male sex: she considers them *to be utterly contemptible and unworthy of notice; to be fickle, false, base, sottish, inclined to perjury, and wholly undeserving.* It's inevitable, therefore, that she should get some sort of comeuppance by falling for a man who won't give her the time of day. If you've received an unwelcome compliment, quote her words with a simper and a modest turning away of the face, flutter an eyelash or two and you may just get away with it.

Parting is such sweet sorrow ...

... That I shall say good-night till it be morrow.
Romeo and Juliet again – the end of the balcony scene, in which the two lovers have (at some length) declared their mutual adoration and are now (at even greater length) trying to tear themselves away from each other. In modern life this just means 'Goodbye' and sounds a bit silly if you say it in anything other than in a jokey tone.

Shall I compare thee to a summer's day? ...

... Thou art more lovely and more temperate
The opening lines of Shakespeare's sonnet number 18 make a charming compliment to pay to a loved one. Beware, though: the closing lines are just a touch conceited, as Shakespeare goes on to boast that his poem will give his beloved eternal life:

> *So long as men can breathe, or eyes can see,*
> *So long lives this, and this gives life to thee.*

You can always hope that your beloved doesn't know this, or, if necessary, deny that you knew it either.

The silent, unfancied majority

A moment of sadness from the lawyer and (frequently very funny) writer John Mortimer; the full quotation, from his autobiography *Clinging to the Wreckage*, is:

No power on earth, however, can abolish the merciless class distinction between those who are physically desirable and the lonely, pallid, spotted, silent, unfancied majority.

He obviously felt strongly about the subject: *Clinging to the Wreckage* was published in 1982 and seventeen years later Mortimer wrote in the *Observer*:

Beauty is handed out as undemocratically as inherited peerages, and beautiful people have done nothing to deserve their astonishing reward.

When it came to his first profession, however, he was more pragmatic. His play *A Voyage Round My Father* contains the observation:

No brilliance is needed in the law. Nothing but common sense, and relatively clean fingernails.

And, in the words of his most famous character, the ageing barrister Rumpole of the Bailey, he wrote about his experiences in the hope of giving *some sort of entertainment to those who, like myself, have found in British justice a life-long subject of harmless fun.*

For someone else who got harmless fun out of British justice, see page 138: A LACK OF SPIRIT ONLY TO BE ADMIRED IN SHEEP.

There is a charm about the forbidden that makes it unspeakably desirable

This is the American author Mark Twain on the perversity of human nature. He obviously gave a great deal of thought to forbidden fruit. In *The Tragedy of Pudd'nhead Wilson* (PUT ALL YOUR EGGS IN THE ONE BASKET – AND WATCH THAT BASKET, see page 28), he also wrote:

> Adam was but human – this explains it all. He did not want the apple for the apple's sake, he wanted it only because it was forbidden. The mistake was in not forbidding the serpent; then he would have eaten the serpent.

'Tis better to have loved and lost than never to have loved at all

Alfred, Lord Tennyson, wrote this in his poem *In Memoriam,* which mourns the early death of his dear friend Arthur Hallam. He meant it sincerely: even amid the worst of his suffering, he is glad to have felt the peaks and troughs of emotion. He might not have expressed it as blatantly as Coco Chanel (see next entry), but he'd have agreed with her sentiments.

To be contented? That's for cows

Couturier Coco Chanel is best known as the creator of 'the little black dress' and, as you might expect, most of her *bons mots* are about fashion. On that subject, she knew her stuff: you can't argue with *Fashion fades, only style remains the same* or *Dress shabbily and they remember the dress; dress impeccably and they remember the woman.* When it came to her private life, though, she was on shakier ground: *Passion always goes and boredom stays* has an air of disillusion about it. Happiness, she maintained, was not a characteristic of a European.

That said, there's an appealing headstrongness about the line quoted above: worth using, perhaps, if you are a person of strong enthusiasms and someone is advising you against throwing yourself into a new and reckless project or love affair.

5

ALL THE VIRTUES I DISLIKE AND NONE OF THE VICES I ADMIRE

Insults, compliments and boasts: smart and witty things to say when you want to be rude, polite or just plain pleased with yourself.

❦

Age cannot wither her, nor custom stale her infinite variety

A very fine compliment, if you can manage to say it without your tongue sliding into your cheek. It's from Shakespeare's *Antony and Cleopatra* and it is part of a long and rapturous description of the Egyptian queen, explaining why Antony is never going to leave her: you get tired of other women, the speaker says, but not this one – you just want her more and more. But see page 92, MY SALAD DAYS, WHEN I WAS GREEN IN JUDGEMENT, for confirmation that this will all end in tears.

All kings is mostly rapscallions

This is said by Huckleberry Finn in Mark Twain's novel, though to be fair he does add, *as fur as I can make out*. Twain was obviously not a fan of royalty – he also wrote:

> *A monarch, when good, is entitled to the consideration which we accord to the pirate who keeps Sunday School between crimes; when bad, he is entitled to none at all.*

And, in *A Connecticut Yankee at King Arthur's Court*:

> *I urged that kings were dangerous. He said, then have cats. He was sure that a royal family of cats would answer every purpose. They would be as useful as any other royal family, they would know as much, they would have the same virtues and the same treacheries, the same disposition to get up shindies with other royal cats, they would be laughably vain and absurd and never know it.*

On the other side of the Atlantic, the British man of letters Horace Walpole had the opportunity to observe both the madness of George III and the shenanigans of his son, the future Prince Regent; he had this to say about royalty:

> *How much on outward show does all depend,*
> *If virtues from within no lustre lend!*
> *Strip off th'externals M and Y, the rest*
> *Proves Majesty itself is but a Jest.*

If you are more in sympathy with royalty than Twain and Walpole, you may like to revert to Shakespeare, who is full of warnings about how hard a monarch's life is. Either:

Uneasy lies the head that wears a crown.

Or:

Falsehood is worse in kings than in beggars.

The first is from *Henry IV Part II*. But the second will *really* impress your hearers: it's not everyone who can quote from *Cymbeline*.

All the virtues I dislike and none of the vices I admire

Winston Churchill said this of the Labour politician Stafford Cripps, who had served in his Cabinet during World War II and went on to be Chancellor of the Exchequer. Churchill gave him several important jobs – including that of negotiating with Stalin – but he obviously didn't like him: he's also quoted as saying of Cripps, *There, but for the grace of God, goes God.*

If Churchill didn't like you, you were in no doubt about it. Many of his most famous insults (*A modest little man with much to be modest about* and *A sheep in sheep's clothing*, both about Clement Attlee, who succeeded him as Prime Minister in 1945) may well be apocryphal, but are worth quoting for all that. Many others can be applied in conversation to anyone you want to be rude about. Can anything be more damning than *In defeat unbeatable, in victory unbearable* – unless it be *He occasionally stumbled over the truth, but hastily picked himself up and hurried on as if nothing had happened*? The former referred to Field Marshal Montgomery, the latter to Stanley Baldwin, British Prime Minister in the 1930s. Even a compliment to a friend came with a barb in it: Churchill said of his ally and fellow wit F. E. Smith: *He had all the canine virtues in a remarkable degree – courage, fidelity, vigilance, love of chase.*

And see page 137, Just like the scent on a pocket handkerchief, for Churchill's particularly dismissive views on Arthur Balfour.

Anyone who extends to him the right hand of fellowship is in danger of losing a couple of fingers

So said Pulitzer Prize-winning journalist Alva Johnston about Fiorello La Guardia, Mayor of New York in the 1930s and '40s (and the man after whom one of the city's airports is named). La Guardia has gone down in history as a reformer who cleared slums, cleaned up parks and broke many of the corrupt practices in the city's politics, even (and I am not making this up) putting paid to a mobster-run racket in the sale of artichokes. But he was not above creating fake budgets in order to make himself look more efficient than he was – and he was bound to make enemies.

The above crack seems to have had no effect on La Guardia's career, but Johnston did bring about the resignation of James Roosevelt, son of President FDR, who was one of his father's most important aides. According to Johnston, the insurance company that 'Jimmy' ran did remarkably well from the business he was able to steer its way. Refraining from any direct accusation, Johnston wrote pointedly: *Some corporations which have given Jimmy insurance have been lucky; some corporations which have denied him insurance have been unlucky.* There is surely an element of 'say no more' about that.

❦

An appeaser is one who feeds a crocodile hoping it will eat him last

This is actually a paraphrase of what Winston Churchill said to the House of Commons in January 1940, during the so-called 'Phoney War': World War II had begun the previous September, but for the first few months so little happened that people genuinely believed it might just go away. Churchill was not one of these optimists: he was First Lord of the Admiralty at the time and a high-profile member of Neville Chamberlain's Cabinet, but he had always been opposed to the Prime Minister's policy of appeasing Hitler. What he said, concerning countries that had remained neutral, was:

> *Each one [of the appeasers] hopes that if he feeds the crocodile enough, the crocodile will eat him last. All of them hope that the storm will pass before their turn comes to be devoured. But I fear greatly that the storm will not pass. It will rage and it will roar ever more loudly, ever more widely.*

The revised version appeared in *Reader's Digest* in 1954, presumably reworded to make it into an elegant, self-contained remark that could be quoted without lengthy explanation. Short and snappy, in other words.

Be it known that you are lofty as the heavens!
Be it known that you are broad as the earth!

Praise indeed. And there's more:

> *Be it known that you destroy the rebel lands! Be it*
> *known that you roar at the foreign lands! Be it known*
> *that you crush heads! Be it known that you devour*
> *corpses like a dog! Be it known that your gaze is*
> *terrible! Be it known that you lift your terrible gaze!*
> *Be it known that you have flashing eyes! Be it known*
> *that you are unshakeable and unyielding! Be it known*
> *that you always stand triumphant!*

Be it known, in other words, that no one should mess with you. Really, seriously, big time, they shouldn't mess with you.

These words appear in a series of hymns dedicated to the Sumerian priestess Inanna, the earliest poems we know of to be ascribed to an author (there is earlier stuff by Anon). They were written by a priestess called Enheduanna, who lived in the 23rd century BC – around 1,500 years before Homer and almost 4,000 years before Shakespeare. That is a long time for any written work to survive. And given that even in Shakespeare's day – and for a good 400 years thereafter – it was always the boys who got the decent education if there was a choice to be made, it's rather fun to discover that Enheduanna, the *earliest ever* known poet, was a woman.

A blackguard whose faulty vision sees things as they are, not as they ought to be

There are many definitions of a cynic, with perhaps the best known being Oscar Wilde's (I CAN RESIST EVERYTHING EXCEPT TEMPTATION, see page 15). But you never know when you are going to need a new one. The above comes from Ambrose Bierce's *Devil's Dictionary*, first published in 1906; if you prefer, use H. L. Mencken's *A man who, when he smells flowers, looks around for a coffin*.

The *Devil's Dictionary* is a rich source of cynical definitions, including:

> *Absurdity: a statement of belief manifestly inconsistent with one's own opinion.*

> *Bigot: one who is obstinately and zealously attached to an opinion that you do not entertain.*

And:

> *Egotist: a person of low taste, more interested in himself than in me.*

But let's give the last word to a man who liked to have the last word, George Bernard Shaw:

> *The power of accurate observation is commonly called cynicism by those who have not got it.*

A Daniel come to judgement!

Shakespeare's *A Merchant of Venice* again (ALL THAT GLISTERS IS NOT GOLD, see page 79): Shylock the money-lender exclaims these words when Portia, disguised as a man of law, agrees that he is entitled to the pound of flesh that Antonio owes him. Portia then turns the tables by pointing out that the agreement says nothing about blood. If, when Shylock cuts into Antonio's flesh, he sheds any blood, all sorts of dire consequences will follow. Antonio's friend Gratiano takes up the refrain (*A Daniel, still say I; a second Daniel*) and Shylock is defeated and humiliated.

In the Old Testament book that bears his name, Daniel is the one who interprets King Nebuchadnezzar's dreams, explains the meaning of 'the writing on the wall' and emerges safely from the lions' den. A versatile fellow. But none of these achievements is relevant here. In the Apocrypha – a collection of books included in some but not all versions of the Bible – Daniel appears in the story of Susanna and the Elders. Two elders lust after Susanna, a virtuous woman; when she refuses them they accuse her of wanton behaviour. Daniel, brought in to judge the case, insists that the two men be questioned separately. Their stories contradict each other, proving that they are lying. So 'a Daniel' came to signify a wise judge – and that is what Shylock means.

The desperate jauntiness of an orchestra fiddling away for dear life on a sinking ship

The American critic Edmund Wilson said this of the style of Evelyn Waugh, author of *Brideshead Revisited*, *Decline and Fall* and many other novels that cast a jaundiced eye on English society in the early to mid-twentieth century. If your first reaction is that Wilson's is an unkind description, read this extract from *Brideshead*:

> *My theme is memory, that winged host that soared about me one grey morning of war-time. These memories, which are my life – for we possess nothing certainly except the past – were always with me. Like the pigeons of St. Mark's, they were everywhere, under my feet, singly, in pairs, in little honey-voiced congregations, nodding, strutting, winking, rolling the tender feathers of their necks, perching sometimes, if I stood still, on my shoulder or pecking a broken biscuit from between my lips . . .*

. . . and you might think that no insult was unkind enough. To do justice to Waugh, not all of his prose is as mannered as that. In addition to being a novelist, he was also a journalist and book reviewer and once remarked:

> *Professional reviewers read so many bad books in the course of duty that they develop an unhealthy craving for arresting phrases.*

So perhaps there is some excuse. He also produced some arresting phrases of his own. Commenting on Nancy Mitford's essay on the English aristocracy, he found one fault with the upper-class family she had created:

> *Surely they should have more children? Impotence and sodomy are socially OK but birth control is flagrantly middle-class.*

On hearing that Randolph Churchill, son of Winston, had had an operation to remove a tumour that proved to be benign, he is also reputed to have remarked something along the lines of:

> *A typical triumph of modern science to find the only part of him that wasn't malignant.*

You can forgive a lot of the man who came up with those two.

The gilded tomb of a mediocre talent

This is how the writer and epigrammatist Logan Pearsall Smith described a best-seller, making it safe to assume that he never wrote one. He was known primarily as a critic – not a career path that often takes you into the best-seller lists – but did well enough at it to be able to observe:

> *How can they say my life is not a success? Have I not for more than sixty years got enough to eat and escaped being eaten?*

Born into a wealthy family in New Jersey and educated at Harvard and Oxford, Smith seems never to have travelled beyond his own country and Europe. Relief at not being eaten is therefore less genuine than it might have been in, say, David Livingstone or David Attenborough, but maybe there was a touch of author's vainglory showing through the words. For, as Smith also wrote:

> *Every author, however modest, keeps a most outrageous vanity chained like a madman in the padded cell of his breast.*

✦

The greatest man who ever came out of Plymouth, Vermont

Perfect if you want to damn someone with faint praise, this was said by the American lawyer Clarence Darrow about Calvin Coolidge, President of the USA from 1923 to 1929. Coolidge, the man whose economic policies are generally blamed for the calamitous 1929 Wall Street Crash, was renowned for his taciturnity: he once said that he'd like to be remembered as a former President who minded his own business and, when informed by a vivacious White House dinner guest that she had bet someone she would get at least three words out of him in the course of the evening, reportedly replied, *You lose*. To appreciate Darrow's remark to the full, you need to know that the population of Plymouth, Vermont, in 1930 was 331.

✦

He has a nice smile, but he has iron teeth

A potentially useful variation on the 'iron hand in a velvet glove' cliché, this was said of Mikhail Gorbachev, the last leader of the Soviet Union. Gorbachev's policies of *perestroika* (restructuring) and *glasnost* (openness) went a long way towards ending the Cold War in the early 1990s and made him considerably more popular in the West than any of his predecessors had been. The remark, however, was made by Andrei Gromyko, the foreign secretary whom Gorbachev had sacked and who presumably wasn't one of his admirers.

He's gone to Heaven, no doubt – but he won't like God

Robert Louis Stevenson is reputed to have said this on learning of the sudden death of fellow poet Matthew Arnold. Arnold was known for the instructive nature of his writing, expressing strong opinions on morality, the importance of good conduct and the lack of cultural education in Britain. It's quite likely that he would have disapproved of the way things were run in Heaven.

His imagination resembled the wings of an ostrich

This was the historian Thomas Babington Macaulay (1800–59) on the poet and critic John Dryden (1631–1700). Given that the ostrich is a flightless bird, you might think this was a particularly bitchy remark – to be interpreted as 'his imagination was completely useless'

– and be surprised, when looking at the dates, to find that Dryden had died a century before Macaulay was born. Who would say anything so unpleasant about someone they didn't know and dislike personally?

But then, have a look at a picture of an ostrich with wings outspread – they're substantial and they're very useful for balance when the bird is running. The rest of Macaulay's remark explains it: Dryden's imagination *enabled him to run but not to soar.* So his imagination wasn't useless; it was merely mediocre. Quite unkind, nevertheless.

It's worth noting that ostriches also use their wings as part of their courtship display. You can't help wondering if Macaulay knew that – and if it would have made any difference if he had.

❦

Hot Shame shall burn upon thy secret brow

Want someone to feel really ashamed of themselves? This is a powerful way of expressing it. It comes from Percy Bysshe Shelley's elegy 'Adonais', written in 1821 on the death of his friend and fellow poet John Keats. Keats, of course, died young, and it may be this that pushed Shelley into his rant (in the same poem) against an unnamed critic who had not only savaged Keats' work in his lifetime but, not having a fraction of the deceased poet's talent, lived on to damn the work of others. *Thou noteless blot on a remembered name* is how Shelley addresses this lesser being, threatening him not only with Hot Shame but with Remorse, Self-contempt and a future spent trembling like a beaten hound. It's safe to say that Shelley is annoyed – and that he makes potent use of capital letters.

I don't like her. But don't misunderstand me: my dislike is purely platonic

Attributed to the actor and theatre manager Herbert Beerbohm Tree, father of film director Carol Reed and grandfather of hell-raising actor Oliver Reed. He said it of a lady (for want of a better word) who, he claimed, had *kissed her way into society*. Perhaps he disliked her because she hadn't kissed him.

Tree was another man renowned for his quips: his most famous one is said to have been addressed to a 'motley collection of women' who were to play ladies-in-waiting to a queen in one of his productions:

Ladies, just a little more virginity, if you don't mind.

And, should you think that that might be difficult to work into conversation, there is also this bitter insult of a contemporary playwright:

He is an old bore. Even the grave yawns for him.

Despite this unpleasant remark, Tree was obviously likeable. Oscar Wilde thought so, anyway: he described him as *a charming fellow, and so clever: he models himself on me.* There can surely be no higher praise.

I should, many a good day, have blown my brains out, but for the recollection that it would have given pleasure to my mother-in-law

The mother-in-law joke, characterizing her as fat, ugly, bad-tempered and a nag, was a staple of comedy in the mid- to late twentieth century: the British comedian Les Dawson, for one, would have been lost without it (*I can always tell when the mother-in-law's coming to stay – the mice throw themselves on the traps* was one of his mildest), while in the 1960s American sitcom *Bewitched*, the antipathy between troublemaking mother-in-law Endora and her son-in-law was integral to almost every one of the 254 episodes.

It may come as a surprise to learn that this genre of 'humour' has a pedigree dating back 200 years: the example quoted above is attributed to Lord Byron, who died in 1824. His marriage lasted little over a year and broke up amid accusations of both homosexuality and incest, so it is perfectly possible that his mother-in-law disliked him intensely – and that the feeling was mutual.

Only a generation later, the French novelist Honoré de Balzac was compiling two treatises on marriage, both of which contain substantial sections on dealing with mothers-in-law. Where he got his information is anyone's guess, because he didn't get married until a few months before his death and there is no suggestion that he spent any time in the company of his bride's mother. Nonetheless, he followed the traditional line on the subject:

> *To have one's mother-in-law in the country when one lives in Paris, and vice versa, is one of those strokes of luck that one encounters only too rarely.*

I won't say she was silly, but I think one of us was silly, and it wasn't me

A fine insult from the normally genteel pen of Elizabeth Gaskell, best known as the author of *Cranford*, though this is from another novel, *Wives and Daughters*. It is fair to say that Mrs Gibson, the woman being referred to, is very silly indeed.

❀

I'm not living with you. We occupy the same cage

A spine-chilling description of an unhappy marriage, this is from Tennessee Williams' play *A Cat on a Hot Tin Roof*. The line is spoken by the frustrated wife Maggie and, if that isn't bad enough, she goes on later in the same scene:

> *How long does it have t' go on? This punishment?*
> *Haven't I done time enough, haven't I served my term,*
> *can't I apply for a – pardon?*

As this is early in Act One and her husband's reply is:

> *Maggie, you're spoiling my liquor. Lately your voice*
> *always sounds like you'd been running upstairs to warn*
> *somebody that the house was on fire . . .*

. . . you have a feeling things can only get worse. And you would not be far wrong.

In the 1958 film, Maggie was played by Elizabeth Taylor, who a few years later turned up as another miserable wife – Martha in *Who's Afraid of Virginia Woolf?*, based on the play by Edward Albee. Much of its dialogue consists of husband and wife, growing ever drunker as the play progresses, baiting each other; among Martha's many memorable insults are:

I swear, if you existed, I'd divorce you.

And, when she has goaded her husband into smashing a bottle into the bar to relieve his feelings:

I hope that was an empty bottle, George! You can't afford to waste good liquor, not on your salary!

❦

Just like the scent on a pocket handkerchief

Contemporaries weren't kind to Arthur Balfour, Prime Minister from 1902 to 1905 and later, as Foreign Secretary, responsible for the Balfour Declaration that announced the British government's support for the creation of a national home for the Jewish people. These words were fellow politician David Lloyd George's response when he was asked what place Balfour would have in history. Winston Churchill was even more scathing:

If you wanted nothing done, Arthur Balfour was the best man for the task. There was no equal to him.

Edward Marsh, who was Churchill's private secretary for many years, recalled in his memoirs a conversation over dinner when he accompanied his master on an expedition to Kenya. One of their hosts:

... made us sit up with an epigram: 'getting other people to do one's work, which is the highest form of skilled labour.' Winston was astonished at finding such

> *a gem in the dark unfathomed caves of Kenya – he
> said it was the sort of thing one might expect from a
> man who saw Arthur Balfour every day.*

You don't have to know or care anything about British politics in the early twentieth century to grab hold of these insults and twist them to your own purposes. Here's another: Chips Channon, whom we met under REFORMERS ARE ALWAYS FINALLY NEGLECTED, WHILE THE MEMOIRS OF THE FRIVOLOUS WILL ALWAYS EAGERLY BE READ (see page 72), recorded a comment on a fellow politician who was kind and high-idealed but boring:

> *He had been offered £30,000 per annum to bore the
> channel tunnel.*

That's close to £2 million in today's money, and several decades before the Channel Tunnel was actually bored by more sophisticated machinery.

A lack of spirit only to be admired in sheep

One to use next time you need to justify a difference of opinion in the home: the politician and writer A. P. Herbert used these words to describe what is shown by *the concept of two people living together for twenty-five years without a cross word.*

Herbert wrote a collection of pieces called *Uncommon Law* (televised in the 1960s as *Misleading Cases*), about instances when the law truly was an ass (see page 65). In one of these, debating whether or not marriage, being a lottery, should be subject to the same laws as other games of chance, he wrote:

> *Women complain, in moments of dissatisfaction, that all men are alike, but men complain with equal indignation that no two women are the same, and that no woman is the same for many days or even minutes together. It follows that no experience, however extensive, is a certain guide, and no man's judgement, however profound, is in this department valuable. In all matrimonial transactions, therefore, the element of skill is negligible and the element of chance predominates.*

There's many a married person – of whichever gender – who would agree with him.

Herbert had his views on the media, too:

> *There is something to be said for the view that the ownership or control of two or more newspapers should be scheduled as a Dangerous Occupation under the Factory Acts, since, as a rule, it seems to lead to mania.*

There is, in fact, a great deal in *Uncommon Law* that makes you think, 'Some things don't change.'

❦

The lady's not for turning

Spoken by British Prime Minister Margaret Thatcher in a speech to the Conservative Party Conference in

Brighton in 1980. Her government had been accused by the press of making 'U-turns' in their policies; Thatcher announced, with heavy-handed wit:

> *To those waiting with bated breath for that favourite media catchphrase, the U-turn, I have only this to say: 'You turn if you want; the lady's not for turning.'*

Famed for her lack of sense of humour, she may or may not have been aware that this was a pun on the title of Christopher Fry's 1948 play *The Lady's Not For Burning*, about a woman accused of being a witch. If you choose to use the line yourself as a sign of your own determination, just be aware of the subtext . . .

❦

Like trying to pick up mercury with a fork

. . . which of course can't be done under normal circumstances, as mercury is liquid at room temperature. In 1921, the then Prime Minister David Lloyd George said this about negotiating with Eamon de Valera, first President of the newborn Irish Republic. De Valera is said to have replied: *Why doesn't he use a spoon?*

It wasn't often Lloyd George was flummoxed: nicknamed the Welsh Wizard, he was immensely energetic, intelligent and confident. He was also sufficiently self-aware to acknowledge that, in order to succeed in politics, *You must keep your conscience well under control.* See NO GUILTY MAN IS ACQUITTED IF JUDGED BY HIMSELF for a different opinion on that subject and SHE TOLD ENOUGH WHITE LIES TO ICE A WEDDING CAKE for an observation made about Lloyd George by one of his least fervent admirers (pages 25 and 147).

❖

The louder he talked of his honour, the faster we counted our spoons

This is American philosopher Ralph Waldo Emerson's take on Shakespeare's *The lady doth protest too much* – the more you say something is so, the less people are likely to believe you.

Throughout history, wise writers have told us that honour should speak for itself. Here is the Roman senator Cato the Elder:

> *I would rather men should ask why no statue has been erected in my honour, than why one has.*

And Mark Twain:

> *It is better to deserve honours and not have them than to have them and not deserve them.*

Then there is the composer Ivor Novello, starring in one of his own musicals, which he was also directing. Asked why he hadn't added to this list by giving himself a couple of songs to sing, he replied:

> *Because I would rather people said 'Why doesn't he sing?' than 'Why does he sing?'*

The writer of light and sometimes schmaltzy romantic musicals echoing one of the sternest Stoics of Ancient Rome? Strange but true.

A man who knows the way but can't drive the car

This was theatre critic Kenneth Tynan's definition of ... a critic. He can't have been speaking about himself, because for one thing an excess of modesty wasn't one of his failings, and for another he was a talented writer himself – his diaries and letters are an incomparable record of the theatrical life of his time.

Many people have been dismissive of critics, but perhaps the gold medal in this category goes to the Irish poet Brendan Behan, who memorably likened them to eunuchs in a harem:

> *They know how it's done, they've seen it done every day, but they're unable to do it themselves.*

Endearingly, Behan – a poet, remember – also observed:

> *You wouldn't want to be minding them poet fellows, they're a dangerous clique be the best of times.*

See also page 127: A BLACKGUARD WHOSE FAULTY VISION SEES THINGS AS THEY ARE, NOT AS THEY OUGHT TO BE.

❧

The milk of human kindness

It may come as a surprise to learn that these words are uttered by one of the least kind characters in Shakespeare, Lady Macbeth; less surprising to know that she views it as a weakness: *Yet do I fear thy nature*, she muses of her absent husband, *It is too full o' the milk of human kindness to catch the nearest way*. Meaning, 'You're too nice to commit a murder and make yourself king.' It's the defining speech of Lady Macbeth's character: she wants her husband to hurry home so that she can *chastise thee with the valour of my tongue* – get rid of that milkiness, in other words, and put some strength into him.

To most people, however, being too kind to murder anybody is a good quality and you may choose to use the expression as a compliment.

Nearer the gods no mortal may approach

A useful way of paying someone a fulsome compliment, this is how Edmund Halley (the seventeenth- and eighteenth-century astronomer after whom Halley's Comet is named) described his near-contemporary Isaac Newton. Newton, one of the greatest scientists of all time, was modest about his achievements: the remark *If I have seen further it is by standing on the shoulders of giants* is often attributed to him. In fact, that concept, if not the exact wording, is much older, dating back to the twelfth-century French philosopher Bernard of Chartres and used by various other writers before Newton. The person standing on the shoulders of a giant is often described as a dwarf – someone who wouldn't be able to see very far at all were it not for the great height (and by analogy the great achievements) of the larger person.

No coward soul is mine

Not a vainglorious boast but a peaceful one: these are the opening words of 'Last Lines' by Emily Brontë, written when she knew she was dying of tuberculosis at the tender age of thirty. If this poem is to be believed, she was dying quite contentedly.

The poets have always been strong on soothing words about death. The Elizabethan Edmund Spenser was positively cheerful about it:

> *Sleep after toil, port after stormy seas,*
> *Ease after war, death after life does greatly please.*

While Shelley, in his introduction to 'Adonais', wrote of the Protestant cemetery in Rome where Keats (another victim of tuberculosis) is buried:

> *It might make one in love with death to think that one*
> *should be buried in so sweet a place.*

Perhaps TB is the linking feature, because it also claimed the nineteenth-century British poets William Henley, who described death as *The sundown splendid and serene*, and Elizabeth Barrett Browning (*Knowledge by suffering entereth/And Life is perfected by Death*) and the Russian Anton Chekhov (*Perhaps man has a hundred senses, and when he dies only the five senses that we know perish with him, and the other ninety-five remain alive*). All of them more or less comforting thoughts.

Not even the mention of sage and onions made her suspicious

Beatrix Potter preceded these words with *Jemima Puddle-duck was a simpleton* and by this stage in the story we know that she has been lured, all unsuspecting, into laying her eggs in a fox's den. The story has a less sad ending than it might have done, but the expression remains a quirky way of describing someone who isn't very bright. Even if they aren't a duck.

Oh, my dear, the noise! and the people!

This is generally attributed to the English actor Ernest Thesiger, replying to someone who asked him how he had felt about his time in the trenches in France during World War I. It's since been applied to almost anywhere from Hell to a rowdy pub; use it to describe any occasion you would have preferred to miss.

One may smile and smile, and be a villain

Shakespeare was keen on villains disguising their villainy with a smile: Hamlet speaks these words after discovering that his uncle and stepfather Claudius – *a smiling, damned villain* – has murdered Hamlet's father. Work your way through the tragedies and you'll find plenty more of the same thing. Lady Macbeth advises her husband to:

> *... look like the innocent flower,*
> *But be the serpent under 't.*

And Iago admits that he follows Othello, not:

> *... for love and duty,*
> *But seeming so for my peculiar end*
> *... I am not what I am.*

Richard III comes right out with it and says:

> *I am determined to prove a villain*
> *... I am subtle, false and treacherous.*

And in *King Lear*, the illegitimate Edmund plots the undoing of his legitimate brother Edgar with the battlecry:

> *I grow; I prosper –*
> *Now, gods, stand up for bastards!*

If villainy is what you want to discuss, Shakespeare is your man.

❦

Self-love is the greatest of all flatterers

This is François de La Rochefoucauld, French seventeenth-century man of letters and collector of maxims. A century later, his fellow countryman Voltaire was writing:

> *Self-love is a balloon filled with wind, from which tempests emerge when it is pricked.*

Lest you think that – for any reason – the French have a monopoly on self-love, the English playwright Philip

Massinger called it *a deceiving mirror* and Shakespeare (in a sonnet) described it as *a sin for which there is no remedy*. So whichever side of the Channel you are on, it is to be deplored. The English essayist Francis Bacon perhaps put it most imaginatively when he wrote:

> *It is the nature of extreme self-lovers, as they will set a house on fire, and it were but to roast their eggs.*

❧

She told enough white lies to ice a wedding cake

Married to the early twentieth-century Prime Minister H. H. Asquith, Margot Asquith had a bad word to say about almost anyone. Lady Desborough, about whom this remark was made, was a rival society hostess who was known to have a number of lovers and was presumably adept at tactful dissimulation.

Margot Asquith probably didn't say to the actress Jean Harlow, who persisted in pronouncing her name 'Margotte', *The t is silent, as in Harlow* – this is much more likely to have been said by a 'blonde bombshell' rival of Harlow's, Margot Grahame. But Asquith did say, of the politician David Lloyd George (Just like the scent on a pocket handkerchief and Like trying to pick up mercury with a fork, see pages 137 and 140), that *He couldn't see a belt without hitting below it.* To be fair, this remark was prompted by Lloyd George's having brought about the downfall of H. H. Asquith's government, so this time at least Margot had an axe to grind.

The great Dorothy Parker (Wherever she went, including here, it was against her better

JUDGEMENT, see page 101) obviously didn't like Margot Asquith – or at least didn't like her writing. In a vitriolic review of Asquith's book *Lay Sermons*, Parker wrote:

> *Her perfect confidence in herself is a thing to which monuments should be erected; hers is a poise that ought to be on display in the British Museum ... no matter where she takes off from, she brings the discourse back to Margot Asquith. Such singleness of purpose is met but infrequently.*

It's tempting to wonder if Lady Desborough cut this review out of the *New Yorker* and framed it to hang in her downstairs cloakroom; you could certainly take extracts from it and use them to take someone down a peg or six.

❧

That man's silence is wonderful to listen to

This is the wording that is used in many dictionaries of quotations, crediting Thomas Hardy's novel *Under the Greenwood Tree*. What appears in the book is slightly longer:

> *Ye never find out what's in that man: never ... Close? ah, he is close! He can hold his tongue well. That man's dumbness is wonderful to listen to.*

Read this in a Wessex country accent to appreciate its true sincerity. No one is suggesting that the man being described – Geoffrey Day, father of the flighty heroine – is a bore who is interesting only when he shuts up. No, this is a real compliment. Geoffrey is a man of few words who can pack a lot into his silences. If Hardy's character had read the works of the American novelist Edith Wharton, writing at much the same time, he might have been tempted to quote:

Silence may be as variously shaded as speech.

And see Iris Murdoch's views on silence on page 48: THE BICYCLE IS THE MOST CIVILIZED CONVEYANCE KNOWN TO MAN.

❦

There is no settling the point of precedency between a louse and a flea

Dr Johnson was never slow to disparage anything of which he disapproved. Among his most famous aphorisms are his definition of oats – *a grain, which in England is generally given to horses, but in Scotland supports the people* – and his response when his friend Boswell described going to a Quaker meeting where there was a woman preacher: *A woman's preaching is like a dog's walking on his hind legs. It is not done well; but you are surprised to find it done at all.* The words quoted above were his answer when asked to choose between the merits of two minor poets. If ever you want to be dismissive of two things you think are as bad as each other, you can do it by quoting Johnson.

For more of Johnson's disparagements, see page 152: WHEN HIS PISTOL MISSES FIRE, HE KNOCKS YOU DOWN WITH THE BUTT END OF IT.

❦

The trouble with her is that she lacks the power of conversation but not the power of speech

This line, widely attributed to George Bernard Shaw, is so established that it has been made into a fridge magnet, but it's unclear whether he actually said it and, if so, who he said it about. No matter – it's a good insult, and one that can easily be adapted to non-females.

Many writers have extolled the virtues of conversation. Jane Austen wrote enthusiastically to her sister Cassandra about:

> . . . the pleasures of friendship, of unreserved conversation, of similarity of taste and opinions.

And Dr Johnson thought:

> The happiest conversation [is] where there is no competition, no vanity, but a calm quiet interchange of sentiments.

The author Rebecca West would have none of this. She maintained:

> There is no such thing as conversation. It is an illusion. There are intersecting monologues, that is all.

Bear that in mind next time you find yourself waiting impatiently for another person to finish speaking so that you can leap in with an anecdote or an opinion of your own.

150

A very valiant trencher-man

This is Beatrice's unflattering description of Benedick in Shakespeare's *Much Ado About Nothing*. The two have an ongoing war of words; when a messenger tries to persuade Beatrice that Benedick is a brave soldier, she maintains that the most valiant thing about him is his stomach – he's so greedy that he can eat even the mouldy food soldiers are fed in wartime. Over the years the phrase has lost Beatrice's sarcastic tone: you could use it simply as a term of jocular approval for someone with a hearty appetite.

Well done, thou good and faithful servant

A slightly patronizing or jokey way of saying, 'Well done', particularly if someone has done you a favour. It's not sarcastic in the Bible (Matthew Chapter 25), however; it is the highest praise. It comes in the Parable of the Talents, where a talent is not an innate ability but a sum of money. The story is that a wealthy man embarking on a journey gives his three servants differing numbers of talents to look after while he is away. Two of them trade with them and make a profit – these are the *good and faithful* servants, whose master rewards them abundantly on his return; the third servant buries his to keep it safe, makes no profit and is abused for being *wicked and slothful*. The message is to use your talents wisely, even adventurously. Otherwise, like the over-cautious servant, you risk being cast out into the outer darkness, where there is *weeping and gnashing of teeth*. And you don't want that.

When his pistol misses fire, he knocks you down with the butt end of it

This is what Dr Johnson did, according to the eighteenth-century Irish playwright Oliver Goldsmith: it meant there was no arguing with him – and certainly no way that Johnson was ever going to admit defeat. Johnson introduced the impoverished young Irishman to London literary circles and became something of a mentor to him, allowing Goldsmith to see through the gruff exterior: *He hath nothing of the bear but his skin*, Goldsmith wrote later.

Their admiration was mutual: after Goldsmith's premature death, Johnson wrote the epitaph that appears on his memorial in Westminster Abbey and described him as *touching nothing that he did not adorn ... vivid, versatile, sublime*. Except, of course, being Johnson, he wrote it in Latin.

One further word from Oliver Goldsmith. In his novel *The Vicar of Wakefield*, the title character Dr Primrose explains the approach that led him to his happy marriage:

> *I chose my wife, as she did her wedding gown, not for a fine glossy surface, but such qualities as would wear well.*

See page 68, NO MAN IS AN ISLAND, for more about the transitory nature of beauty.

You have delighted us long enough

Mary in Jane Austen's *Pride and Prejudice* is the third of the five Bennet daughters and the only plain one. (Yes, it's bad that that mattered so much, but the girls' only hope of a comfortable future was a 'good' marriage – there's no denying that beauty helped.) Mary, therefore, had acquired 'accomplishments' to make up for what she lacked in looks; with them she had, unfortunately, acquired some unattractive habits: *A pedantic air and conceited manner, which would have injured a higher degree of excellence than she had reached.*

Small wonder, then, that at an evening party when it looks as if Mary will go on singing all night, her father utters the immortal but damning words:

> *That will do extremely well, child. You have delighted us long enough. Let the other young ladies have time to exhibit.*

Probably better, if you want to use the expression yourself, to turn it into the first person: '*I* have delighted you long enough' is a good way of excusing yourself from further showing off; saying it in the original form to someone else is hardly kind.

You're a better man than I am, Gunga Din!

A useful remark if you think someone has done something praiseworthy (or if you think they have been just a tiny bit rash). It comes from a poem by Rudyard Kipling, in which Gunga Din is the regimental *bhisti* or water-bearer, an important figure for soldiers in India. The point of the poem is to praise the efforts of this ragged but brave and compassionate man, who runs around the battle lines ministering to the wounded and dying. The last line of the poem – *You're a better man than I am, Gunga Din!* – is completely sincere, with no trace of the sarcasm that usually accompanies it when it is quoted out of context.

The poem also describes Gunga Din in a word that no logophile should be without: *Lazarushian-leather*. The reference is probably not to the Lazarus who came back from the dead, but to one in another Biblical story, a beggar who died neglected at a rich man's gate and was subsequently taken up to Heaven. It's reasonable to imagine that Gunga Din's skin was both leathery and 'covered in sores', as Lazarus's was – and that Kipling's narrator imagines that he, too, will have his reward in another life.

6

THERE IS MUCH PLEASURE TO BE GAINED FROM USELESS KNOWLEDGE

A mishmash of wise words on some practical and impractical aspects of life: the arts and the sciences, war, peace and politics.

❀

The ballot is stronger than the bullet

This isn't exactly what Abraham Lincoln said, in a speech in 1858, but it is the substance of what he meant. The longer version is:

> *To give victory to the right, not bloody bullets, but peaceful ballots only, are necessary.*

You can see why someone came up with a shorter, brisker version . . .

A lot of worthy things have been said in favour of voting and democracy. Winston Churchill, for example, put a case for it in 1947:

> *No one pretends that democracy is perfect or all-wise. Indeed, it has been said that democracy is the worst form of government except all those other forms that have been tried from time to time.*

George Bernard Shaw, never one to let an occasion for cynicism go unacknowledged, remarked that:

> *Democracy substitutes election by the incompetent many for appointment by the corrupt few.*

Perhaps the best definition comes from the American satirist H. L. Mencken, whom we met under LOVE IS THE DELUSION THAT ONE WOMAN DIFFERS FROM ANOTHER (see page 112):

> *Democracy is the theory that the common people know what they want, and deserve to get it good and hard.*

See also page 166: IN POLITICS SHARED HATREDS ARE ALMOST ALWAYS THE BASIS OF FRIENDSHIPS.

Be less curious about people and more curious about ideas

Marie Curie apparently spoke these words to a reporter who was looking for an interview with her and her husband, fellow scientist Pierre Curie: mistaking Marie for the housekeeper, he asked if she could share any gossip about the couple and got this no-nonsense reply.

Marie Curie's list of achievements is extraordinary. Not only could she send impertinent journalists away with fleas in their ears, she was also the first woman to win a Nobel

Prize, the first person and only woman to win twice and the only person to win for two different sciences – physics and chemistry. All of this happened in the first two decades of the twentieth century, when 'woman' and 'science' were not words usually found in the same sentence. She was also the first woman to have her ashes enshrined in the Panthéon in Paris, an honour previously reserved for the 'great men' of France. Although her work with radiation caused frequent bouts of ill-health (and her papers are still, more than eighty years after her death, too radioactive to be handled by anyone not wearing protective clothing), her love of science never diminished. Her sayings on the subject include:

> A scientist in his laboratory is not only a technician: he is also a child placed before natural phenomena which impress him like a fairy tale.

And:

> Humanity needs practical men, who get the most out of their work, and, without forgetting the general good, safeguard their own interests. But humanity also needs dreamers, for whom the disinterested development of an enterprise is so captivating that it becomes impossible for them to devote their care to their own material profit.

The origin of the idea that, if you choose a job you like, you'll never work a day in your life is generally attributed to Confucius, but if Marie Curie didn't say it, she easily could have done.

❦

C'est magnifique, mais ce n'est pas la guerre

This translates as 'It's magnificent, but it isn't war', but it somehow loses its oomph if you say it in English. It's an observation made in 1854 by the French general Pierre Bosquet on the Charge of the Light Brigade – a notorious incident during the Crimean War. It's usually quoted in this form, omitting the concluding words that make it into a sensible remark: *C'est de la folie* – it's madness.

And indeed it was madness. Alfred, Lord Tennyson, tried to romanticize it in his poem 'The Charge of the Light Brigade', which begins:

> *Half a league, half a league,*
> *Half a league onward,*
> *All in the valley of Death*
> *Rode the six hundred.*

And includes the famous lines:

> *Theirs not to reason why,*
> *Theirs but to do and die.*

But although it appears that the soldiers of the Light Brigade behaved with great courage, their officers were at loggerheads with each other and the best word to describe the way their orders were given is 'shambles'. Of the 650-odd horsemen who charged down the valley, over a hundred were killed and only 195 returned with themselves and their horses unhurt. Whatever Bosquet or Tennyson would have us believe, there was very little about it that was *magnifique*.

Could we teach taste or genius by rules, they would no longer be taste or genius

This is taken from *Discourses on Art* by the painter Sir Joshua Reynolds, who was also the first president of the Royal Academy of Arts. Genius itself, though, is not enough:

> *You must have no dependence on your own genius. If you have great talents, industry will improve them; if you have but moderate abilities, industry will supply their deficiency.*

Reynolds served a three-year apprenticeship with an established artist and then travelled and studied in Europe, so he clearly put his own tenets into practice. Other artists have, on balance, agreed with him. Pablo Picasso was another who believed in hard work:

> *Our goals can only be reached through a vehicle of a plan, in which we must fervently believe and on which we must vigorously act. There is no other route to success.*

Even Salvador Dalí, who called his autobiography *Diary of a Genius* and described himself as *the genius of the greatest spiritual order of our day, a true modern genius*, acknowledged that study played a part:

> *If you refuse to study anatomy, the arts of drawing and perspective, the mathematics of aesthetics, and the science of colour, let me tell you that this is more a sign of laziness than of genius.*

In case you are concerned that this is Dalí showing uncharacteristic signs of either modesty or seriousness, here is a quote more in keeping with his usual style:

Every morning upon awakening, I experience a supreme pleasure: that of being Salvador Dalí, and I ask myself, wonderstruck, what prodigious thing will he do today, this Salvador Dalí.

To keep the confusion going (which is surely what he would have wanted), let us throw in one last Dalí-ism:

It is not necessary for the public to know whether I am joking or whether I am serious, just as it is not necessary for me to know it myself.

Going back to the topic of work, though, if it doesn't appeal you could try quoting the Impressionist Edouard Manet:

It is not enough to know your craft – you have to have feeling. Science is all very well, but for us imagination is worth far more.

Nobody could describe Manet as idle – he packed a lot into his fifty-one years, in terms both of his own work and of his influence on other artists – so you can be confident that quoting him is not taking the lazy way out.

The curious incident of the dog in the night-time

Given wider currency since 2003 thanks to the novel by Mark Haddon and the play based on it, this expression comes from the Sherlock Holmes short story 'Silver Blaze', by Sir Arthur Conan Doyle. Silver Blaze is a racehorse that has disappeared just before an important race; its trainer has been murdered. Holmes, investigating, draws the police's attention to the curious incident of the dog in the night-time:

> 'The dog did nothing in the night-time.'
> 'That was the curious incident,' remarked Sherlock Holmes.

Spoiler alert: the point is that the intruder into the stables was someone the dog knew, so it didn't bark.

'Silver Blaze' also contains the line *A long shot, Watson; a very long shot!*, which Holmes says when a rather fanciful theory turns out to be the correct one. In the novel *The Sign of Four*, he comes out with: *When you have eliminated the impossible, whatever remains, however improbable, must be the truth.* They're both remarks that are worth having in your repertoire for sometime when you have made a lucky guess or have produced a preposterous solution to a problem.

❦

Curiouser and curiouser

Immortal words spoken by Alice (in her *Adventures in Wonderland*, by Lewis Carroll), when she has eaten a cake that makes her grow – *opening out like the largest telescope that ever was*; 'Goodbye, feet!' she exclaims, as they disappear from view.

Curiouser and curiouser are the opening words of Chapter 2 of the book, so you can imagine that there is plenty more to come. Although Alice has already followed the White Rabbit down the rabbit hole and drunk something that makes her shrink to a height of only 10 inches, she doesn't know the half of it – things are going to get a lot curiouser before she gets home again. See page 168: IT'S THE OLDEST RULE IN THE BOOK.

❧

Everyone is a genius at least once a year ...

... A real genius has his original ideas closer together.

These words were uttered by an eighteenth-century German called Georg Lichtenberg, described as a physicist and a satirist – an unusual combination, you might say. You might also suspect that the axiom came under the heading of satire rather than physics and even then that Lichtenberg was probably being generous to most of his fellow human beings. Many of us have never had an original idea, never mind a flash of genius, in our lives. And that is perhaps just as well, if a later satirist, the Englishman Samuel Butler, is to be believed: he maintained that genius might be described as:

> *A supreme capacity for getting its possessors into trouble of all kinds and keeping them therein so long as the genius remains.*

❧

Facts alone are wanted in life

The motto of Mr Gradgrind, superintendent of the school board, in Dickens' *Hard Times*. It occurs in a speech he is making in the very first paragraph of the book, and he goes on:

> *You can only form the minds of reasonable animals upon Facts: nothing else will ever be of any service to them.*

It's no accident that Dickens spells Facts with a capital F, nor that the name of the schoolteacher employed by Mr Gradgrind to suppress anything remotely resembling creativity in his pupils should be M'Choakumchild. You can imagine (providing Mr Gradgrind and Mr M'Choakumchild haven't squeezed that concept out of you) that this approach causes a great deal of misery, even by Dickens' standards; you may prefer the attitude of Albert Einstein, exploding into the scientific world half a century after *Hard Times* was published:

> *Logic will get you from A to B. Imagination will take you everywhere.*

❦

He who has no poetry in himself will find poetry in nothing

This is another maxim of Joseph Joubert (WHAT IS TRUE IN THE LAMPLIGHT IS NOT ALWAYS TRUE IN THE SUNLIGHT, see page 77), who is particularly eloquent on poetry:

> *Poets have a hundred times more good sense than philosophers. In seeking the beautiful, they find more truths than philosophers do in seeking the true.*

It's easy to be high-falutin' about poetry, of course: you can quote John Keats (*If poetry comes not as naturally as the leaves on the tree it had better not come at all*) or the French playwright Jean Giraudoux (*As soon as war is declared it will be impossible to hold the poets back. Rhyme is still the most effective drum*).

Too fancy? Fall back on Dylan Thomas:

> *Poetry is not the most important thing in the world . . . I'd much rather lie in a hot bath reading Agatha Christie and sucking sweets.*

❧

A highbrow is the sort of person who looks at a sausage and thinks of Picasso

A definition that would not have been out of place in Ambrose Bierce's *Devil's Dictionary* (A BLACKGUARD WHOSE FAULTY VISION SEES THINGS AS THEY ARE, NOT AS THEY OUGHT TO BE, see page 127), this was in fact written by the lawyer and politician A. P. Herbert. For more about him, see page 138: A LACK OF SPIRIT ONLY TO BE ADMIRED IN SHEEP.

❧

I don't think we have failed. We have just found another way that doesn't work

This is what aeronautical engineer and balloonist Andy Elson said in 1999 when his attempt to fly round the world in a balloon had to be abandoned. Elson's company had produced balloons and life-support systems for numerous record attempts and research projects, including taking a hot-air balloon to a world-record altitude of more than 21,000 metres (70,000 feet) over Mumbai; he himself piloted one of two balloons to make the first balloon flight over Mount Everest. Clearly, as the song suggests, he's someone who can pick himself up, dust himself off and start all over again.

Ernest Rutherford, physicist and atom-splitter, had a pragmatic slant on a similar problem:

> *We haven't got the money, so we've got to think!*

❧

I would rather fail gloriously than dingily succeed

Bloomsburyite Vita Sackville-West wrote these words in a 1928 letter to Virginia Woolf, pondering whether it was better for the novel she was planning to be *extremely ambitious or rather modest*. The latter may be safer, but her hatred of safety brings her to the conclusion quoted above. The Australian writer Ambrose Pratt took the opposite view:

> *I would rather be a philosopher and a coward than a hero and a fool.*

If you couple these with the opinions expressed under AVOIDING DANGER IS NO SAFER IN THE LONG RUN THAN OUTRIGHT EXPOSURE (see page 81), you should have most options covered on the subject of safety or risk.

In a single stroke with a medium-grained nail file you could eradicate human history

You're probably familiar with the idea that, if you think of the history of the Earth as being a 24-hour day, humankind turns up a few seconds before midnight, like the guest at a New Year's Eve party who arrives just in time for 'Auld Lang Syne'. Well, the above is an alternative, proposed by the Pulitzer Prize-winning writer John McPhee in his 1981 book *Basin and Range*. Stretch your arms out to your sides as far as they can go, he suggests, and imagine that distance as the length of the Earth's life; then get out that nail file and remind yourself just how insignificant we are.

❧

In politics, shared hatreds are almost always the basis of friendships

The idea that 'My enemy's enemy is my friend' is as old as the hills – or at least as old as the *Arthashastra*, a treatise on statecraft written in Sanskrit about 2,500 years ago. This wording comes from the nineteenth-century French diplomat and social historian Alexis de Tocqueville, best known for his study of *Democracy in America*. He obviously gave a certain amount of thought to the role of hatred in politics, because he also wrote:

> *A despot easily forgives his subjects for not loving him, provided they do not love each other.*

De Tocqueville's fellow countryman, the philosopher Voltaire, no lover of despotism, expressed a somewhat extreme view:

> *The best government is a benevolent tyranny tempered by an occasional assassination.*

For other views on forms of government, see page 155: THE BALLOT IS STRONGER THAN THE BULLET.

It is when I am struggling to be brief that I become unintelligible

This is a confession made by the Roman poet Horace in his influential work 'Art of Poetry': whenever a poet strives to do something, he fails. Someone trying to be sublime becomes bombastic, while those who err in the other direction *creep along the ground like a wretched reptile*. Do what comes naturally, is Horace's message: as he puts it (bizarrely, you might think), it's no good being able to draw a cypress tree if you're being paid to paint a sailor swimming desperately away from a shipwreck.

Brevity in particular has been recognized as a problem for writers for many centuries. The French mathematician Blaise Pascal wrote in the seventeenth century that *I have made this a long letter because I didn't have time to write a short one* and Mark Twain wrote much the same thing 200 years later. When Woodrow Wilson, President of the United States during World War I, was asked how long it took him to prepare a speech, he replied:

That depends on the length of the speech. If it is a ten-minute speech it takes me all of two weeks to prepare it; if it is a half-hour speech it takes me a week; if I can talk as long as I want to it requires no preparation at all. I am ready now.

It's the oldest rule in the book

Again from Lewis Carroll's *Alice's Adventures in Wonderland* and again connected with Alice's growing (CURIOUSER AND CURIOUSER, see page 161). She is a witness at the trial of the Knave of Hearts (accused of stealing tarts) and has unaccountably grown large again, leading the King of Hearts, who is presiding over the court, to scribble in his notebook and then proclaim:

'*Rule Forty-two. All persons more than a mile high to leave the court.*'

> *Everybody looked at Alice.*
> '*I'm not a mile high,*' *said Alice.*
> '*You are,*' *said the King.*
> '*Nearly two miles high,*' *added the Queen.*
> '*Well, I shan't go, at any rate,*' *said Alice; 'besides, that's not a regular rule: you invented it just now.*'
> '*It's the oldest rule in the book,*' *said the King.*
> '*Then it ought to be Number One,*' *said Alice.*
> *The King turned pale and shut his note-book hastily. 'Consider your verdict,*' *he said to the jury, in a low trembling voice.*

There's no outwitting Alice, even in a court of law in Wonderland. Back in the real world 'the oldest rule in the book' can be used to describe any rule, whether it's a reasonable one that deserves to be Number One or an idiotic suggestion that deserves to be as far down the list as Number Forty-two.

❧

The life of man, solitary, poor, nasty, brutish, and short

This may sound as if it belongs in the chapter on the meaning of life, but in fact it is Thomas Hobbes' argument against war in general and civil war in particular. Hobbes was a hugely influential English philosopher of the seventeenth century and this line comes from his masterwork *Leviathan*. He refers to the circumstances in which *Every man is Enemy to every man* and precedes the words quoted above with this terrifying description:

> *In such condition, there is no place for Industry; because the fruit thereof is uncertain; and consequently no Culture of the Earth; no Navigation, nor use of the commodities that may be imported by Sea; no commodious Building; no Instruments of moving, and removing such things as require much force; no Knowledge of the face of the Earth; no account of Time; no Arts; no Letters; no Society; and which is worst of all, continuall feare, and danger of violent death.*

Given that Hobbes was writing during the Commonwealth which followed the English Civil Wars and the execution of Charles I, this was both a controversial and an extraordinarily courageous anti-war stance.

❧

Like a drug, the machine is useful, dangerous and habit-forming

When George Orwell wrote this in *The Road to Wigan Pier* in the 1930s, he was talking about the sort of machine that put miners and farm labourers out of work; he went on to say:

> *You have only to look about you at this moment to realize with what sinister speed the machine is getting us into its power.*

Little did he know that in the early years of the twenty-first century we would be laughing at the man who had said (in the 1970s) that no one would ever need a computer in the home, and making movies about robots taking over the world and committing crimes. As the science-fiction author Isaac Asimov, writing in the latter part of the twentieth century, put it:

> *The saddest aspect of life right now is that science gathers knowledge faster than society gathers wisdom.*

For other things that Orwell thought he was making up, see page 49: BIG BROTHER IS WATCHING YOU.

❧

The most beautiful things in the world are the most useless . . .

. . . peacocks and lilies, for instance.

This is the Victorian art critic John Ruskin, speaking in praise of beauty. An eager disciple of Ruskin's, William Morris, leading light of the Arts and Crafts Movement, allowed for a little more practicality:

> *Have nothing in your houses that you do not know to be useful, or believe to be beautiful.*

That was Morris's 'golden rule', established in *Hopes and Fears for Art* (1882). He led up to it with something that is perhaps even more relevant to those who find it hard to throw anything away:

> *If we want art to begin at home, as it must, we must clear our houses of troublesome superfluities that are forever in our way: conventional comforts that are no real comforts and do but make work for servants and doctors.*

In these servantless days it might be more relevant to change that last bit to *just give you something else to dust*, but the principle is the same.

Music, when soft voices die, vibrates in the memory

If you know nothing about music but want to make an appreciative remark, there is no shortage. This is a particularly poignant one, from a poem by Shelley that is generally known by this, its opening line, and has often been set to music.

Also in the poignant category is:

Musick has Charms to sooth a savage Breast.

These are the opening words of *The Mourning Bride*, a 1697 tragedy by William Congreve. They're so well known that you might like to add a touch of erudition by continuing with the second line:

To soften Rocks, or bend a knotted Oak.

But if you know the context, you might not find this as soothing as you'd hoped: the lines are spoken by the mourning bride of the title, and what she's saying is that she must somehow have become less sensitive than trees or rocks, because the music isn't soothing her at all.

A point for the trivia buffs, though: *The Mourning Bride* contains another line that has become almost a proverb. Although the original is longer, it is usually paraphrased as:

Hell has no fury like a woman scorned.

Nothing to do with music, obviously, but it may prove useful in other circumstances.

Almost as famous is the opening line of Shakespeare's *Twelfth Night*:

If music be the food of love, play on.

But this, too, has negative undertones: the lovelorn Orsino wants the musicians to play on so that he has too much of it and *The appetite may sicken, and so die.*

If you just want to convey that the music is lovely, Shelley is probably your best bet here.

Nature red in tooth and claw

A handy remark when you've been watching a particularly gory wildlife programme on television. It's from Tennyson's poem 'In Memoriam' ('TIS BETTER TO HAVE LOVED AND LOST THAN NEVER TO HAVE LOVED AT ALL, see page 119) and it comes in a section about Man trusting in God's love despite the evidence of Nature's brutality that he sees all around him. Tennyson wonders if we will all end up being *blown about the desert dust*.

Probably, is the gloomy answer. So it's perhaps easier just to quote it out of context, sticking to the wildlife programmes rather than delving into deeper questions of metaphysics.

❧

No poems can live long or please that are written by water-drinkers

The Roman poet Horace liked his wine: his works are full of references to the god Bacchus and to Falernian cheer, Falernian being the great wine of his day. In this instance, however, he is quoting the Athenian comic writer Cratinus – not approvingly, but to make a point. Cratinus had made this remark 500 years earlier, and ever since, Horace says, poets have become drunkards because they think that this will make them good poets. It's nonsense. True talent lies in originality, not in copying anything about your predecessors, particularly their drinking habits. That may be so, but it's unlikely that much of Horace's work was written under the influence of water.

It was also he who coined the expression *Carpe diem* – 'seize the day' – in one of his odes, advising us that:

> *Even while we speak, hostile Time will have been*
> *running away.*
> *Seize the day and trust as little as possible to*
> *tomorrow.*

There was no ice cream in Ancient Rome (though a hundred years after Horace the Emperor Nero was sending slaves into the mountains to collect snow which was then eaten flavoured with fruit – an early sorbet). But had he lived in the twentieth century, Horace would surely have enjoyed the American playwright Thornton Wilder's attitude to seizing the day:

> *My advice to you is not to inquire why or whither, but*
> *just to enjoy your ice cream while it's on your plate.*

The idea of living life now because you're a long time dead has inspired other poets and philosophers, too: *Up, sluggard, and waste no life; in the grave will be sleeping enough* is how Benjamin Franklin (THREE MAY KEEP A SECRET, IF TWO OF THEM ARE DEAD and WHAT IS THE USE OF A NEW-BORN CHILD? see pages 75 and 179) put it, while it was the theme of a whole poem by Andrew Marvell, addressed 'To His Coy Mistress' and encouraging her not to delay having sex with him because:

> *At my back I always hear*
> *Time's wingèd chariot hurrying near.*

In other words, time is running out, let's get on with it. There's a lot more on the same theme, including the suggestion that once the woman is dead the worms *shall try that long preserved virginity.* Whether she succumbed to this somewhat unromantic argument is not recorded.

❧

Some circumstantial evidence is very strong, as when you find a trout in the milk

When Thoreau wrote this in his journal (on 11 November 1850), it made little sense, because nothing he had said before or after was anything to do with evidence. Or trout. Or milk. Never mind – readers picked up on it. The line became sufficiently familiar for it to feature in a case in the Court of Appeals of Georgia in 2009. A woman was suing the company that had serviced the air-conditioning unit in the shop where she worked, because she had subsequently been poisoned by the carbon monoxide it released; the judge's summing up included these words:

> *'Some circumstantial evidence is very strong, as when you find a trout in the milk,' Henry David Thoreau's allusion to the practice of some dairymen of watering down milk ... If you find a fish in your milk, it is reasonable to conclude the dairyman added water to it, for how else would a fish get there? Here, if you find carbon monoxide gas in your store after the technician services your air conditioner ... it is reasonable to conclude that the technician caused the carbon monoxide emission.*

You don't have to go to court to use this expression; it's a picturesque substitute for 'This is obviously the answer, even if we don't have concrete proof.' Or *res ipsa loquitur* – the thing speaks for itself – as Latin scholars would say.

❦

There cannot be a crisis next week. My schedule is already full

These words of American politician Henry Kissinger were quoted in the *New York Times Magazine* on 1 June 1969, only months after he had become United States National Security Adviser under President Richard Nixon. And we can all sympathize with how he felt, whether or not our jobs involve us in issues of world peace. Even at this early stage in his career, Henry had established a talent for 'Kissingerisms' – a sidebar in the magazine article quotes several, including the one given above and:

> *The pre-eminent task of American foreign policy ought to be to get some reputation for steadiness. Whether we are dangerous to our enemies one can argue, but we are murder on our friends.*

Perhaps not meaning to be taken seriously, he's also been known to remark:

> *Seen one President, seen them all.*

Fifty years later, it might be interesting to ask senior White House officials if they agreed.

❦

There is much pleasure to be gained from useless knowledge

History does not record whether or not the philosopher and mathematician Bertrand Russell was an aficionado of pub quizzes, but he'd obviously have been a great success at them. He wrote these words in a collection of essays called *In Praise of Idleness*, having considered the idea a few years earlier in *The Conquest of Happiness*:

> *To be able to fill leisure intelligently is the last product of civilization.*

A great humanitarian and politically a socialist, Russell was from an aristocratic background and, when he was approaching sixty, was embarrassed to inherit an earldom on the death of his brother. After instructing his publishers that he didn't want the title to be used in connection with his literary work, he added:

> *There is, so far as I know, only one method of getting rid of it, which is to be attainted of high treason, and this would involve my head being cut off on Tower Hill. This method seems to me perhaps somewhat extreme.*

If you like the sound of this man, take a look at his views on being buried with honours under AN ATHEIST IS A MAN WHO HAS NO INVISIBLE MEANS OF SUPPORT and on human misery under THE BICYCLE IS THE MOST CIVILIZED CONVEYANCE KNOWN TO MAN (pages 46 and 48).

There's husbandry in heaven . . .

. . . their candles are all out.

In other words, the gods are being economical and have turned out the lights. There are no stars to be seen. This comes from Shakespeare's *Macbeth* – Banquo (whom Macbeth will murder and who will turn up as a ghost at a banquet later in the play) says it when he is wandering around Macbeth's castle at night, unable to sleep: he has a premonition that something bad is about to happen. He's right, of course – Macbeth disappears offstage to stab Duncan in the very same scene.

You needn't wait for an imminent murder to use this, though: it's just a casual observation to make on a very dark night.

❧

Wars begin when you will, but they do not end when you choose

The Florentine politician Niccolò Machiavelli made this indisputable point in his account of the history of Florence, and it applies to more than wars: it's a sophisticated way of saying, 'Look before you leap.'

Machiavelli was full of sound advice for anyone not over-burdened with idealism: one of his best-known maxims was *It is much more secure to be feared than to be loved* and, although it's a bit long for working into most conversations, there's a strong element of common sense in:

> A man who wishes to make a profession of goodness in everything must necessarily come to grief among so many who are not good. Therefore it is necessary for a prince who wishes to maintain himself, to learn how not to be good, and to use this knowledge or not use it, according to the necessity of the case.

As for wars not ending when you choose, the Frenchman Alexis de Tocqueville (IN POLITICS, SHARED HATREDS ARE ALMOST ALWAYS THE BASIS OF FRIENDSHIPS, see page 166), writing a generation after his own country's revolution, had this to add:

> In a revolution, as in a novel, the most difficult part to invent is the end.

Be warned.

<hr/>

What is the use of a new-born child?

This is the unanswerable retort the American polymath Benjamin Franklin is said to have made when someone wondered what was the use of a new invention. A century later, British scientist Michael Faraday quoted Franklin in an address to the City Philosophical Society in London, deploring the attitude of those who were in the habit of asking what was the use of any new fact. He was able to give a more specific response to the Prime Minister, William Gladstone, when the latter asked about the usefulness of electricity:

> Why, sir, there is every possibility that you will soon be able to tax it.

Wonder is the feeling of a philosopher, and philosophy begins in wonder

Spoken by Socrates, written down by Plato in the fifth century BC, this thought is remarkably similar to one expressed by Ralph Waldo Emerson over 2,000 years later:

Men love to wonder, and that is the seed of science.

You might like to compare Emerson's thought with what Marie Curie had to say about science (BE LESS CURIOUS ABOUT PEOPLE AND MORE CURIOUS ABOUT IDEAS, see page 156) and Albert Einstein about imagination (FACTS ALONE ARE WANTED IN LIFE, see page 162). These super-brainy people, whether they were scientists or philosophers or a bit of both, had a surprising amount in common.

❧

You may drive out Nature with a pitchfork, yet she still will hurry back

Two thousand years ago, the Roman poet Horace, a keen gardener, recognized that his hobby required hard work, and these words of his have been echoed by horticulturalists down the ages. In the twentieth century, the influential English gardener Margery Fish advocated knowledge of the tasks in hand and firmness in carrying them out:

Plants are like babies – they know when an amateur is handling them.

But gardening also seems either to inspire an optimistic outlook on life or to attract people who have one already: those who write about it are always looking to the future and wondering what a new season will bring. The great twentieth-century garden designer Gertrude Jekyll wrote – in England, where February can be a miserable month:

> *There is always in February some one day, at least, when one smells the yet distant, but surely coming, summer.*

And:

> *A garden is a grand teacher. It teaches patience and careful watchfulness; it teaches industry and thrift; above all it teaches entire trust.*

The writer Vita Sackville-West (I WOULD RATHER FAIL GLORIOUSLY THAN DINGILY SUCCEED, see page 165) created the magnificent gardens at Sissinghurst Castle in Kent, and she was always looking forward to the next exciting occurrence:

> *No gardener would be a gardener if he did not live in hope.*

And:

> *The most noteworthy thing about gardeners is that they are always optimistic, always enterprising, and never satisfied. They always look forward to doing something better than they have ever done before.*

Despite the greatness of her achievement at Sissinghurst, she remained modest about it:

The more one gardens, the more one learns. And the more one learns, the more one realizes how little one knows.

You could probably use any or all of these as a metaphor for life. Or just talk about gardening. Entirely up to you.

Sources

Many of the quotations in this book were gleaned from *The Oxford Dictionary of Quotations, The Oxford Dictionary of Quotations by Subject, The Oxford Dictionary of Modern Quotations* and Dr Laurence J. Peter's *Peter's Quotations for Our Time*. Among the numerous websites that offer quotes from every source or for every occasion, brainyquotes.com, wikiquote.org and goodreads.com filled in a number of gaps, while quoteinvestigator.com is excellent on questions along the lines of 'Did Mark Twain (or Madame de Staël or Margot Asquith) *really* say this?' Project Gutenberg (gutenberg.org) provides searchable text of Horace, Shakespeare, Thomas Hardy, Charles Dickens and many more, which enabled me to fit a quotation into its context; sparknotes.com and cliffsnotes.com give handy tips on what these people were talking about; and poetryfoundation.org helped me to find out more about Christina Rossetti and the wombat (see page 82: BETTER BY FAR YOU SHOULD FORGET AND SMILE THAN THAT YOU SHOULD REMEMBER AND BE SAD).

Information given under BE IT KNOWN THAT YOU ARE LOFTY AS THE HEAVENS! BE IT KNOWN THAT YOU ARE BROAD AS THE EARTH! (see page 126) and the translation of Enheduanna's writing came from Black, J. A., Cunningham, G., Fluckiger-Hawker, E., Robson, E., and Zólyomi, G., *The Electronic Text Corpus of Sumerian Literature* (http://www-etcsl.orient.ox.ac.uk/), Oxford 1998–.

The story about Fiorello La Guardia and the artichokes (see page 124: ANYONE WHO EXTENDS TO HIM THE RIGHT HAND OF FELLOWSHIP IS IN DANGER OF LOSING A COUPLE OF FINGERS) was taken from Michael Pye's masterly 'biography of New York', *Maximum City* (Sinclair-Stevenson, 1991).

Edward Marsh's *A Number of People* (Heinemann, 1939) gave me not only the story quoted under JUST LIKE THE SCENT ON A POCKET HANDKERCHIEF (page 137), but also Bertrand Russell's remark about chocolate-creams (see page 49: THE BICYCLE IS THE MOST CIVILIZED CONVEYANCE KNOWN TO MAN) and Ivor Novello's explanation of his not singing (see page 141: THE LOUDER HE TALKED OF HIS HONOUR, THE FASTER WE COUNTED OUR SPOONS). Thank you to my favourite magazine, *Slightly Foxed*, for publishing the article by Derek Parker (in *SF*57) that steered me towards that delightful book.

Index

187